A Natural Approach

to

Mental Wellness

by Gregg Krech

ToDo Institute

Monkton, Vermont

\

Dedicated to David K. Reynolds,

whose work has made a significant difference

in many peoples' lives

ToDo Institute

P.O. Box 50

Monkton, Vermont 05469

Copyright © 2000, 2008, 2011 by Gregg Krech.

2nd Printing June - 2000

3rd Printing - 2002 (revised edition)

4th Printing - 2008 (revised edition)

5th Printing – 2011 (new revised edition)

All Rights Reserved.

(802) 453-4440

todo@todoinstitute.com

www.todoinstitute.org

ACKNOWLEDGMENTS

Much of the material in this book draws on the principles of several methods of Japanese approaches to mental health. Shoma Morita, M.D., developed Morita Therapy and Ishin Yoshimoto developed the method of self-reflection called Naikan. David Reynolds, Ph.D., was primarily responsible for importing these methods to North America and adapting them for Westerners. My teachers in Japan, Rev. Shue Usami, Akira Ishii, Mrs. Yoshimoto and Mr. Nagashima, graciously allowed me to learn from them. I have also been influenced by the work of Thich Nhat Hanh, Eknath Easwaren, Linus Pauling and Abram Hoffer, M.D., who established the connection between nutrition and mental health. And finally, by Richard Leider, who offers great wisdom for finding purpose, and Viktor Frankl, whose profound work in Logotherapy emphasized the importance of meaning and purpose in one's life. Special thanks to Nancy Newlin, who did a fine job of editing and proofreading the final manuscript and to Sue Cole who reviewed the section on self-reflection. And my heartfelt thanks to my wife, Linda Anderson Krech, who generously acts as my editor, proofreader, colleague, teacher and friend. Her patience and constant support are invaluable.

Thank you all.

TABLE OF CONTENTS

INTRODUCTION

S uppose you wish to learn to play the piano. Many pianists begin playing when they are children, but you can still learn to play even if you're retired. Of course you will need to find a piano teacher and, most importantly, you will need to practice. Practice may involve playing scales and doing certain finger exercises. As you learn, you work on progressively more difficult compositions. While you practice, you translate what you know intellectually into skills. Practice is bodylearning. Your fingers and hands learn new ways of moving and coordinating movement with one another. After you have learned some basic skills you can enjoy playing different kinds of music. But without these skills you'll be very limited in what you can do.

The same thing is true in basketball and most other sports. I've coached young girls, ages eight to twelve. Initially their connection with the basketball is awkward and clumsy. They have to learn basic skills like dribbling with both hands, passing, shooting, rebounding and, of course, defense. Once these skills are absorbed they start playing naturally. They have the capacity to play quickly and gracefully.

Mental wellness also requires skill. We usually don't think of mental health as an area that requires us to learn skills. But if you have seen a therapist you may have already learned some skills. The skills you have acquired depend on how you spent time in the sessions and what kind of therapy you were in. Here are some of the skills you may have already learned:

1. Problem solving

2. Showing up on time for appointments

3. Expressing your feelings to others

4. Blaming others for your problems

5. Selectively focusing on the problems and difficulties in your life

6. Getting in touch with unpleasant and painful feelings

7. Talking about yourself

8. Analyzing yourself ("why do I do what I do?, why am I the way I am?")

I don't believe the last five skills have much to do with mental wellness. In fact, they have much more to do with suffering. Those people we admire for their accomplishments, their character and their compassion for others, are not likely to have developed these skills. The first two skills on this list -- problem solving and timeliness -- have some value and relationship to mental wellness. They are skills worth developing and worthy of continued practice.

So what skills are required for mental wellness? There are many skills that will have a good influence on your mental health such as problem solving, time management, organizing your living space, and managing your finances. Guidance on these topics is readily available. The four skills I would like to identify, however, are indispensable to mental wellness and rarely discussed. They are also skills in which many of us are deficient. And the absence of even one of these skills can result in a great deal of suffering for us and those around us. Let's explore these skills one by one.

Skill #1

ACCEPTANCE

A monk asked Master Dongshan,

"Cold and heat descend upon us. How can we avoid them?"

Dongshan answered, "Why don't you go the place where there is no cold or heat?"

The monk continued, "Where is the place where there is no cold or heat?"

Dongshan said, "When it is cold, let it be so cold that it kills you. When it is hot, let it be so hot that it kills you."

Generally, when we are in conditions that we find unpleasant we try to manipulate the conditions so they align with our own preferences and desires. If it is hot, we put air conditioning in our homes and cars. If it is humid, we use a dehumidifier. If it is cold, we turn up the furnace so we're nice and toasty and don't venture out unless we have to. If we're alone and it's too quiet, we play some music in the background.

When we find ourselves in situations that stimulate emotional discomfort, we also try to manipulate the situation so we will feel better. We often use one of the following three strategies:

AVOIDANCE

This involves trying to escape from our feelings/thoughts --
avoiding what is uncomfortable and pursuing what is
comfortable. We may try to "cheer up" or take a bath to help
us feel relaxed. We may watch TV or recite affirmations.
Regardless of the method, our goal is to replace discomfort
with comfort. This is a goal shared by many forms of
contemporary psychotherapy. We want to feel confident,
relaxed, and happy. The avoidance strategy involves
resistance. We resist our emotional experience and devote
great energy and attention to trying to manipulate ourselves
into a different state. Unfortunately, the resistance itself
nurtures our discomfort. And the preoccupation with our
internal experience (thoughts and feelings) tends to intensify
our suffering while distracting us from activity that can give
our life meaning and purpose.

RESIGNATION

We may accept our emotional state and take no action
whatsoever. This is a type of acceptance that is really
resignation. It is what happens when the depressed person
realizes that he or she is depressed and then continues to lie on
the sofa all afternoon in a state of melancholy. Takehisa Kora,
M.D. (a prominent Morita therapist) uses the Japanese term
"*akirame*" to characterize this approach, and differentiates it
from Morita's idea of acceptance which goes beyond inactive
resignation. In resignation, we are not trying to escape from
our feelings, we are simply languishing in them.

COMPLAINING

On a hot summer day I asked my seven year old daughter,

"Who is hotter -- a person who constantly complains throughout the day about how hot it is or a person who doesn't complain?"

She said the person who complained would be hotter. When I asked her why, she said, "Because he would feel hotter." When we grudgingly accept our circumstances, we may nevertheless continue to resist our experience by regularly complaining. We may accept that it is hot, and we may continue to go about our work, but our experience is punctuated by complaint after complaint which reminds others how uncomfortable we are and reminds ourselves how much we wish things were different than they are.

"Paradoxically, this practice of complaining increases clients' suffering. The more they detail their complaints, the more they focus their attention upon the complaints."

- Shoma Morita, M.D.

There is a fourth strategy for dealing with our emotional discomfort which I would like to introduce:

ARUGAMAMA

Arugamama is the term that psychiatrist, Shoma Morita, used to describe the true state of acceptance. It means "to accept things as they are." It comes closest to Dongshan's advice in the Zen koan described earlier. When we are hot, we just let ourselves be hot. When we are anxious, we just let ourselves feel anxiety. When we are depressed, we just allow ourselves to feel depressed and hopeless. The state of arugamama is one in which we do not try to escape from our emotional experience. We are not seeking any kind of emotional or cognitive state other then the one we are in at the moment. Yet we continue to devote ourselves to what it is that is important for us to do. We carry out the purposes of our lives, because they give life meaning.

In arugamama we find the quality of non-resistance, similar to what is taught in many forms of martial arts. When our opponent is bigger or stronger, direct resistance is ineffective. So we learn to use our opponent's energy against him. Through non-resistance, a small person can defeat a larger and stronger person. Through non-resistance, a weak-willed person can defeat anxiety or depression. It is not necessary to conquer or overpower our depression. We accept the experience of depression and make no effort to escape. And we invite depression to accompany us while we make dinner, or go shopping or walk our dog. Depression is our companion as we make our public presentation.

Most of the tasks and challenges we face stimulate mental and emotional processes. Fear, anxiety, boredom, frustration or lack of confidence may accompany us at any time. Of course, we often idealize what this internal experience should be. "I shouldn't be so afraid of such things." "I shouldn't be so anxious about this presentation." When we are so caught up in our idealized views about how we should be, we cannot accept things as they are. It is like the monk saying, "It shouldn't be so hot. It's already September." But at this moment it is this hot. It's just as hot as it is. So to practice this state of arugamama we have to allow the heat to "kill" us. This doesn't mean that we literally die. It means that we are consumed by the heat to such a degree that we are completely hot. There is no resistance, no complaint, no effort to escape. The Buddhist teacher Pema Chodron has written a book called *The Wisdom of No Escape.* What a wonderful title (and a wonderful book, too).

> *"Resistance is the fundamental operating mechanism of what we call ego – resisting life causes suffering."*
>
> *- Pema Chodron*

At one point in my life I was facing a great dilemma. Through a series of foolish choices I had created a situation so that no matter what choice I made next, I would create great suffering for someone, as well as for myself. For months I refused to accept the reality of this situation and struggled for a way out, an escape that would be free of suffering. But I couldn't find such a solution. My clever mind, which had served me so well in the past, could not find a way out. No matter which way I turned, I would encounter, and cause, a great deal suffering. So I remained paralyzed -- trapped by inaction and constant rumination. Then one day it hit me: Suffering was inevitable. There was no escape. I accepted this premise, not just intellectually, but with my whole being. There was no escape! And when I realized this, I took action. I took the next step. Of course, pain and suffering followed. But I was able to accept the situation as it was. And I've had to live with the karma that I created. But life had to continue, to move forward. Arugamama allows us to move forward, because we are consumed by the heat, consumed by things as they are. When we stop trying to escape from things as they are, we can move forward and live in a more natural and meaningful way.

What will you do with the summer heat? Accept it or resist it? What will you do with your anxiety? Accept it or struggle with it? What will you do with your sister, who constantly criticizes you, and your mother who incessantly complains? Will you accept them or struggle to fix them? Are there things in life worth struggling for? How can we discover what they are?

Generally, we think of acceptance as being in opposition to action. But Morita's view of acceptance is that it is an important element of action. In fact, we might say that acceptance of our internal human condition, as well as external conditions -- is at the very heart of action.

THE ACCEPTANCE OF OTHERS

The value of acceptance goes far beyond acceptance of our thoughts and feelings. Most strong willed people consistently try to control the external conditions of life. In some cases, these external conditions can be controlled but in many other cases (for example, the weather) they cannot. Perhaps most common is our tendency to try to control other people -- what they do, what they think of us or how they feel. To be honest, this effort to try to control others often gets us into trouble. So we need to learn the wisdom and skill of simply accepting what is. Life cannot always be the way we want it to be. Our plans rarely go according to plan. Flexibility and acceptance are qualities that help us live more wisely -- spiritually as well as psychologically.

> *"People who believe they can change or control everything are usually in a great deal of pain, because this is simply not possible."*
>
> *- Dzigar Kongtrul Rinpoche*

A few years ago, my family and I took a trip to Costa Rica, where we explored the natural wonders of this extraordinary country. We had a four-wheel drive car, luggage, two children, a dear friend, and often no plans beyond the current day. As our journey unfolded I found myself increasingly trying to control our daily affairs. My basic motivation was to keep all of us safe and healthy and have an enjoyable trip. But I was trying to impose my own ideas of how things should unfold -- where we should stay, what roads to take, what restaurants to eat at and what places to explore. Rather than enjoying the trip as it naturally unfolded I was trying to get it to unfold according to my wishes. My effort to control our situation was causing me a lot of stress, and it was also creating a great deal of tension between me and my family members.

So one night I announced to my wife that I would just stop this. I made the next day an "acceptance day." I deferred all decisions to my wife or my children. The only element of will power I exerted was in a situation where personal safety was an obvious issue (like a rip tide at the beach). Initially, I found myself struggling to accept things that went against my own mental desires and preferences.

But as the day wore on I found myself relaxing into this experience and enjoying our trip much more than on previous days. I learned (or relearned) that things could progress in a way that was different from my ideas and still work out nicely. What a surprise!

Much of the suffering that occurs in relationships is related to our efforts to try and control other people. The alternative is to accept them as they are -- an option which is much more compatible with loving them. When we stop trying to fix or change the other person, it frees up our energy to just love them.

"When I truly accept something, I am no longer invested in making it different. I may still share my opinion. I may even indicate that I would prefer things to be otherwise, but I don't become invested in trying to make it so. There's more of a lightness. I recognize that the world, including my partner, does not exist for my pleasure and convenience. My partner is not me. The more we can embrace the whole package, the more loving we can be."

- Linda Anderson Krech

HOW DO WE LEARN ACCEPTANCE?

This is one of the most common questions I am asked. There are certain logical paths to developing many skills and they all involve practice. But how do you practice acceptance? Though it is a challenge, it is possible to develop the capacity to be a more accepting person. The ways of practicing involve the options of (1) working on yourself from the outside in, and (2) working on yourself from the inside out. The first approach involves a focus on controlling one's behavior. The second method involves coming to a different understanding of our circumstances and the limitations of our ability to control our lives.

Most of life is outside our control. We go through life trying to control the way it unfolds, but it takes only a short period of time before something happens that shows us that we simply can't control life. To be skillful at acceptance doesn't mean to go through life passively. There are many times when we must try to influence situations around us. But the person who has the capacity for acceptance is not attached to control. He is not attached to the outcome of his efforts. He recognizes that he must make a sincere effort to influence certain situations, yet, underlying his actions is the awareness that there are numerous karmic factors that play a part in how life evolves, and one's own efforts play only a small part in the outcome. Having the capacity for acceptance does not make us a doormat. We can possess qualities of action, persistence and determination. But we start with the "acceptance of things as they are." This is always where we begin. We encounter life with a sense of humility based on an honest appraisal of our limitations and fallibility. *We don't always know what is best.* Sometimes life (or God, Buddha or some Higher Power) has a better idea of what needs to happen than we do.

Practice

1.   **Acceptance Day**

This is probably the best single exercise for developing the capacity for acceptance. It is an exercise about giving up control – giving up one's willpower. The stronger your will, the harder it will be to do this exercise successfully. To practice this exercise it is best to work with a partner, a spouse or someone you will spend most of the day with. You can even do it with your children. You agree in advance that the other person will have control of the decisions and choices for the day. It's that simple. They decide what to have for dinner, what route to take to the store, what movie to rent, or how long to stay sitting at the dinner table. If you want to really challenge yourself, you can even have the other person pick out your clothes and select your food, and portions, for each meal. Your job is to simply accept the decisions or plans that are made by your partner. Just go along with EVERYTHING! You can watch your mind disagree and argue, but don't allow those thoughts to migrate into your speech. Allow the day to unfold -- participate, but don't direct.

2.   Meditation

Meditation provides an opportunity to simply notice and accept the inner workings of your mind. For twenty minutes, just sit and follow your breath. Follow the breath coming in. Follow the breath going out. Breathe deeply, but try to refrain from controlling the breath. Just allow yourself to be breathed. As you do this your mind will wander and various thoughts will arise. As you become aware of those thoughts, just accept them and bring your attention back to your breath. Do the same thing with any feelings that arise. Notice, accept and return to the breath.

3.   Self-reflection

In one of the later chapters of this book I describe an approach to self-reflection called Naikan. Naikan provides a structure, using a series of three questions, with which you can reflect on a relationship, an event, or a period of time. Naikan is a method that can help us to accept situations and people, as well as ourselves. Please read the section on Self-reflection for a more detailed explanation of Naikan.

Resources

Krech, Gregg. Naikan: *Gratitude, Grace and the Japanese Art of Self-reflection* (Stone Bridge Press)

Miller, Daniel. *Losing Control, Finding Serenity*. (Ebb and Flow Press)

Skill #2

Co-Existing with Unpleasant Feelings

"When we accept our emotions as they come, we develop an attitude of openness -- we can make friends with our emotions and allow them to travel their natural course. Once we adopt this attitude of openness and receptivity, we see everything, in a sense, as perfect."

- Tarthang Tulku

Have you ever introduced yourself to someone at a party even though you felt shy and uncomfortable doing so? Have you ever gone walking or jogging even though you felt lethargic and unmotivated? Have you ever given a speech or presentation even though you felt anxious and self-conscious? In each case you had to act in a way that was inconsistent with very uncomfortable feelings. Since you didn't, or couldn't, get rid of these feelings, you had to take them along for the ride. This is called coexisting with unpleasant feelings.

In the last chapter we discussed the skill of acceptance. Sometimes the wisest choice is to simply accept what is. But in many cases, we need to go beyond acceptance and respond to the situation. Acceptance is the first step – responding is the second step. In reality, these two steps are not separate, but merged into a seamless response. However, our response can be hindered by our feeling state.

Many of us have spent much of our lives responding to our feelings with action or inaction -- whatever our feelings might dictate at the moment. If we feel like eating dessert, we eat dessert, even though we're trying to lose weight. If we don't feel like exercising, we stay in and watch TV instead. *Coexisting with unpleasant feelings* is the antithesis of such a feeling/response approach. In some cases it means coexisting with anxiety about a presentation you need to make even as you stand up and begin speaking (coexistence/action). In other cases it means coexisting with anger while you refrain from hitting someone or from yelling at them (coexistence/restraint). Both aspects of this skill involve the ability to feel what you're feeling, think what you're thinking, and observe and accept the content of your feelings and thoughts without being drawn into an automatic reaction, which is often typical of emotionally charged situations.

What I'm describing can generally be considered self-discipline or self-control. The ability to coexist with feeling states is the foundation of self-control, but it is truly a skill, not just an idea. You develop this skill the same way you learn to play the piano, by practicing. How do you practice? Well, life will give you many "exercise" periods each day, sometimes when you least expect them. You come home from work and find that your dog has urinated on the carpet. You return to your car in the parking lot and find that someone sideswiped you and left a dent in the passenger door. Maybe you're having some medical tests done and you're waiting for the results. You practice coexistence by learning to work with these everyday situations without allowing your body (behavior) to automatically respond to your internal experience (feelings/thoughts). Most of us have some skill in this area but the more a situation stimulates strong emotions and thoughts, the closer we get to our "edge" -- the point at which the demands of the situation surpass our ability to handle the situation wisely. If we can continue to work at our edge our skills may develop further and fewer situations will either provoke or paralyze us.

Our feelings are feelings.

Our actions are actions.

The space in between

is our freedom.

THE STRENGTH OF NON-RESISTANCE

Generally, we don't like to feel unpleasant feelings or think disturbing thoughts. When we feel upset, frustrated or depressed, we may encounter those feelings with a response of "I don't like to feel this way. I want to feel differently." On the surface, this seems like a reasonable response. Many individuals seek therapy in an effort to change the intensity or content of their feelings and many therapists, in turn, work toward helping their clients "feel better." But by struggling with our feelings, we are practicing resistance rather than acceptance. This process sets the stage for a growing resistance to our feeling states as we try to fix, change, and transform the feelings that we don't like into feelings that we do like. The more we resist or fight these feeling states, the stronger they become. It's as if the attention we give to unpleasant feelings is actually a form of nourishment, like water to a plant. The more we try to "work on" or "work through" such feelings, the more they grow, branch out, and occupy a larger space in our life.

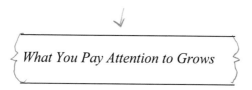

What You Pay Attention to Grows

The alternative is to encounter these unpleasant feelings (I don't refer to such feelings as "bad", only unpleasant) with acceptance. This doesn't mean you like feeling depressed or enjoy feeling anxious; it just means that you accept the reality that you are feeling depressed.

At this particular moment, I feel depressed.

And you don't direct your energy towards trying to change, or work on, your feelings. You just notice them and accept them. There is a wonderful blues song with the lyric, "Good morning blues, blues how do you do?" Imagine greeting your feelings of depression by saying "Good Morning" and asking your depressed feelings how they're doing. In musical form, this is an illustration of non-resistance.

Suppose you are planning to play tennis or golf on Sunday morning, but when you wake up the sky is enveloped in black clouds and it is raining. It continues to rain steadily as the time approaches for your game. You feel disappointed. You were really looking forward to playing this morning, but now you can't. You may look out the window from time to time to check the weather, but after a while you accept the reality of rain and begin making other plans. It would be foolish to stare at the clouds for hours and mentally try to make the rain stop. We know there is nothing we can do about the rain, so we reach a state of acceptance naturally and relatively easily. We would be wise to treat our feelings this way as well. Give up on them. Stop trying to manipulate them. Accept their natural fluctuations and redirect our energy, knowing that feelings pass just as the clouds pass overhead.

Arugamama is a Japanese term that describes a state of acceptance. When feelings are accepted, our energy can be fully directed to taking action. The action itself is likely to influence our feelings as in a situation where we feel lethargic and unmotivated and yet we participate in a yoga class or a basketball game. After a few minutes we may find that our feeling state has changed and we feel exhilarated or energetic. This shift in our feelings is not necessarily predictable or controllable, yet it's a good example of the body/mind principle at work. Some researchers would explain the subsequent shift in feelings by pointing out that taking action often stimulates a series of biochemical changes involving hormones, neurotransmitters, blood pressure, etc . . . We can study such changes that are surfacing in the newest research on the topic of neuroplasticity. But we don't need to understand the biochemistry of the body and brain to experience the changes taking place.

WHAT ABOUT THOUGHTS?

We have been discussing the acceptance of feelings, but thoughts can be treated the same way. Like feelings, they simply arise. They are beyond our control. The Zen Master

Kosho Uchiyama wrote a wonderful essay about thoughts, referring to them as "secretions in your head."

"You might try looking at all the stuff that comes up in your head as just a secretion. All our thoughts and feelings are a kind of secretion. It is important for us to see that clearly. I've always got things coming up in my head, but if I tried to act on everything that came up, it would just wear me out."

- Kosho Uchiyama Roshi

Some people believe it is a good idea to accept their feelings, but they resist accepting their thoughts -- particularly thoughts that are self-blaming, judgmental, perverted, or otherwise unpleasant. But why try to change your thoughts? Why not just notice them and let them go on their way? If you try to control your thoughts you have to constantly watch them, like being in charge of a group of toddlers. "Hey, don't do that. Hey, get back over here. Please don't put that in your mouth." People who try to change their thoughts have to live like this. Even if you have some success, it wears you out -- it absorbs much of your energy. But if you accept your thoughts as secretions, you can put all that energy into actually living your life. Your thoughts just come along for the ride.

"When you try to stop your thinking,

it means you are bothered by it.

Do not be bothered by anything."

- Shunryu Suzuki Roshi

The Uncertain Future

Often, when we are in an emotionally agitated state, our minds begin to create scenarios of the future. These scenarios are often based on fear or hope. For example, a young woman ends the relationship with her long-term boyfriend and imagines that she'll never meet anyone and fall in love again. She begins to have thoughts of herself as aging, childless and without an intimate partner. She feels an increasing level of distress, fear and sadness. In another situation, a man is passed over for a promotion. Though disappointed and angry, he begins to see himself leaving the company and getting a job with a competitor. He hopes his new job will have higher status and more pay and his mind reassures him that he is competent and headed for professional and personal success.

Both individuals are grasping for some certainty in a future which is, by definition, uncertain. We cannot know what the future will bring. Our challenge is living with the present, acknowledging that we don't know what is going to happen later. We only know the reality of the state of affairs we are faced with now. If we can stay grounded in what is knowable, we can avoid being drawn into the thoughts, dreams, fears and images of an unpredictable future. Our situation is like a chapter in a book. We haven't finished the book yet. We're not supposed to know how it ends. But by moving forward, page by page, word by word, we will discover what happens next.

THE COMFORT ZONE

Who doesn't like to be comfortable and safe? How sweet are those moments in which we're cozy and relaxed, not challenged by temperature, hunger, thirst, mosquitoes, noise, biting wind, pain, or anxiety. But when comfort becomes our guiding principle in life, we are in jeopardy of losing our vitality and purpose. In the quest to keep our personal world safe and predictable, and in our effort to avoid discomfort and challenge, we are also limiting ourselves. Rather than taking steps to address our challenges and build our dreams, we avoid and procrastinate. We don't make efforts to meet a new partner, work on our tax return, or find a different job – and gradually the comfort in this zone starts wearing thin. How ironic that through our efforts to remain within our comfort zone, we eventually create a very uncomfortable place to live.

When we're floating in the comfort zone, we don't need to adapt very much to conditions and circumstances. But when we pierce through the comfort cocoon in order to accomplish something meaningful, beautiful, or important to us, we must adapt to the needs of the situation. Not only do we accomplish that which needs to be done, but we become stronger, wiser and more capable, as well.

Rowing across the Atlantic was, without a doubt, the hardest thing I've ever done. I wanted to get out of my comfort zone, and that, by definition, is an uncomfortable place to be. Physically, it was tough, but psychologically it was even tougher. The ocean is scary and it's daunting and most of the time I wanted to give up.

But no matter how hard it got, I always believed that the only thing worse than carrying on would be to quit.

I believe that if you don't keep pushing the boundaries, keep expanding your comfort zone, your comfort zone actually gets smaller and smaller, until you're shrink-wrapped in such a tiny comfort zone that you can't move, you can't achieve anything, you can't grow. And so I keep pushing, keep developing, keep evolving. I keep showing what an ordinary person can do when they put their hearts and minds and souls into it.

- Roz Savage

Expressing Feelings

Sometimes talking about your feelings can help you to accept them, particularly feelings which are very unpleasant or uncomfortable. Conventional psychotherapy often suggests that expressing your feelings allows you to "get them out." – release them, somehow. This approach suggests that if we talk about our feelings enough we can get rid of them – exorcise them. *But when we speak we are letting out words, not feelings.* And there is no convincing evidence that feelings are transformed in any kind of permanent way by expressing or identifying them. In fact, many people find that repeatedly talking about feelings such as depression, anxiety or anger can not only keep those feelings alive, but stimulate even more intense feelings of a similar nature. Complaining makes us good at complaining. Yelling makes us good at yelling. So instead of "releasing" feelings we find ourselves more overwhelmed by our feelings than before.

Of course, if we want to stimulate certain feelings, like love or passion, expressing those feelings may help. For example, I may tell my wife I love her or let my mother know that I am grateful for what she has done for me. This can be a healthy and purposeful way to communicate love or gratitude.

But when we repeatedly talk about our unpleasant feelings, it is easy to fall into the habit of simply complaining and wanting our suffering to be the center of attention. This isn't characteristic of mental wellness and often disregards the impact our words have on those around us. It is best if we can cultivate the skill of acceptance of feelings first. Then, if we wish to talk about our feelings from time to time it is not done out of some desperate need to fix, release, or work on our feelings.

LEADING WITH THE BODY

One of the central principles of Morita Therapy is that we have much more control over the body (actions) than the mind (feelings/thoughts). During long meditation periods I would find that my mind would be all over the place – "I wonder what's for lunch today?" "I wish I would have slept better last night." "I hope everything is OK at home." But I could keep my body relatively still during the same period. Off of the cushion, I've found that I could eat a bowl of beet soup (Beets are one of my least favorite foods) even as my mind was saying, "Yuk, beets are totally disgusting." When you're angry, you can have the thought, "I'm going to kill this person," and not actually attack them with your fists or a weapon. We don't realize how much control we have over our body, because we don't pay much attention to how often the content of our mind is out of sync with our actions. If we acted on every thought or feeling we had, our lives would be utter chaos.

Of course, you can't always control the body, particularly if your body is medically or physically incapable of a particular action. No amount of willpower will allow me to jump six feet in the air from a standing start. Nor can a person who is paralyzed from an accident stand and walk across the room through sheer effort. There is a gray area, however, when it comes to many health and mental health problems. A young man who is severely depressed may report that he simply "can't get out of bed." A woman with mononucleosis may claim that she really can't walk up and down the stairs. In what situations is the body physically incapable of performing a task, and in what situation is it simply due to lack of effort, self-discipline, willpower or the lack of skill in coexisting with our feelings?

During one of our long Vermont winters, I had a severe case of the flu. For a few days I found that I needed an inordinate amount of rest and I would feel exhausted even after the slightest physical effort. When I was laying down, my body felt achy, heavy and tired and I would have the thought, "I just can't get up right now." If someone else reported this to me, I might be skeptical. I might think, "Well, you probably could get up if you really had to." So this was a very humbling experience for me.

As I lay in bed, I continued to experiment with my situation and I stumbled upon a technique that can be very helpful when we need to get our bodies moving. I found that the best way to get myself up was to start with small muscle movements and then gradually work towards larger and larger muscles. So while lying down, I would start wiggling the end of my index finger and then gradually expand that movement to all the fingers on both hands. Then I would wiggle my toes. Next I would lift my left arm slightly and then both arms. Then rotate my shoulders and maybe lift a leg. At that point, I could usually swing my legs over the side of the bed or sofa and stand up. Once I was up, it was easy to take a few steps. The more I would move around, the easier it was to keep moving. We might call this the law of momentum – it's easier to keep going once you've started than to get started in the first place. This is generally true of exercise programs, diet, writing, public speaking – almost anything. It's a bit like warming up the engine in your car before you start driving.

The best way to create momentum is by taking small steps. This strategy is well documented in a Japanese approach called Kaizen. Kaizen began as a method of continuous improvement in the manufacturing industry, but its application to personal change has been developed by Robert Maurer, a therapist, who suggests that small steps are the key to accomplishing change over time. Small steps give us momentum, yet only require a minimum of effort. If you want to exercise, begin by just walking around your house. If you want to write a novel, just write for five minutes a day. If your house is a total mess, start by just cleaning one corner of one room.

As you are anticipating your action, your thoughts and feelings are likely to offer resistance. But remember, you don't need to go along with them. And you don't need to try to motivate yourself or change your thinking. You just need to coexist with your internal experience while you put on your shoes and walk for two minutes. Once it becomes clear to you that this is possible, you'll find that the skill of coexisting with your feeling state is tremendously empowering. You no longer have to feel like doing something in order to do it.

Remember when you first learned to walk – to take those first few steps from point A to point B. Well, you probably don't remember and neither do I. But if you see a baby who is just learning how to walk, you can see the excitement on her face. "Wow, I can get from here to there and nobody has to carry me. And I can do it whenever I want to do it. I don't have to wait for someone else." Discovering that we can coexist with our feelings (and thoughts) while we take action is an exciting discovery! It empowers us to move forward with our life without waiting for our internal experience to change. It's not hard to take action when you are motivated, enthusiastic, and energized. Most of us can do that. But we can't remain in that state forever, just as we can't expect the tide to always be in, or the sun to always be out. Life is a dynamic flow – in an out, up and down. By learning to take action when we don't feel like doing something, we overcome anxiety, fear, and depression without overcoming them at all. We are no longer slaves to our feelings. With this skill, we have purchased our freedom and now can choose a path guided by purpose and the needs of the situation, as it arises -- moment by moment.

OCHO: OVERCOMING BY GOING AROUND

The other day I was walking down our driveway, which had become icy as a result of sleet, freezing rain, a warm sun, and then cold frigid temperatures. One large segment of the driveway was like a skating rink. Even if you walked very carefully, it was almost impossible to cross the ice without slipping and falling. So I decided to simply go around the ice by walking alongside the driveway where there were still several inches of crusty, hard snow. By going around the ice, I was able to continue my walk without confronting the ice directly.

This is the strategy Morita therapy offers for dealing with the challenging feeling-states we all face from time to time -- depression, fear, anxiety, despair, frustration and even anger. We are generally taught that we must face our problems and confront them directly. This can work well when the problem is a car that won't start or weeds in your garden. You get in there and work hard on the problem until it is solved. But this doesn't work very well when the "problem" is our feeling-state. For this problem, we may be better off learning how to "overcome by going around."

"There is an old Buddhist term, ocho, which means overcoming by going around. In confronting a problem head-on, you may encounter a wall so high and thick that you cannot break through it. So you turn to one side and go around the wall. This is ocho. Instead of sitting desolately in front of the wall that is blocking your progress, you try to get around it by making a long detour, or even by digging under it . . . It is a subtle but simple movement of the mind that makes this transformation complete, but an invaluable one to learn and perfect."

- Hiroyuki Itsuki

It takes a lot of strength to knock down a wall of depression. It takes great courage to break through a wall of fear. But to simply go around the wall doesn't require any strength or courage at all. It requires a bit of wisdom. It requires clarity of purpose. And it requires acceptance. We leave the ice intact. We leave the wall standing. We overcome our anxiety by going around it, not by destroying it or freeing ourselves from it. You don't need to travel in a straight line. Water doesn't travel in a straight line. Because of its flexibility it is impossible to contain it. Let us learn the art of *ocho* and live more like water.

The Dinner Party

At last the night of Mrs. Davis' dinner party had arrived. She had been carefully planning it for almost a year. Everybody who was anybody was going to be there. Clearly this was the event of the year in Roseville.

In spite of all her planning, Mrs. Davis still had dozens of things to do. The hors d'oeuvres hadn't been prepared and the good china teacups were still in storage boxes. The rug needed to be vacuumed one more time and she hadn't yet done her hair. She wanted the evening to be a smashing success.

As she sliced the olives she heard a knock on the door. Who could that be? Probably someone collecting for some charity. Wiping her hands, she peered out the window at her front porch and was horrified! What are they doing here? She didn't invite them. She felt devastated, for knocking relentlessly at the door was Mr. Depression and his wife Mrs. Anxiety.

What could she do? If she let them in they would ruin everything. They would keep her from finishing her preparations and her party would be a failure. Maybe she could just ignore them, pretend they weren't there. Of course it wasn't polite, but it would serve them right for showing up at such an inopportune time.

So she began unpacking her china teacups and ignoring the persistent knocking. But try as she may, she could still hear them. "Oh go away," she said to herself. "I can't hear you. You're not there."

Her valiant efforts were failing. The knocking got louder and louder. She couldn't shut out the sound. She began noticing the tension in her stomach and shoulders. The knocking got so loud it sounded as if the door was about to be smashed to pieces. Poor Mrs. Davis B what else could she do? She just didn't have the time to entertain her unwanted guests. There was too much to do. But this wasn't working either.

Then she had a brilliant idea. "What if I let them in, tell them to make themselves at home and continue preparing for the party?" she thought. "Could it work? Dare I try it?" To be sure, they will not be pleased. Each previous visit Mr. Depression and Mrs. Anxiety demanded Mrs. Davis' full attention. They would want tea and cakes and conversation. She had always thought she had to attend to them. She never dreamed of letting them in and continuing to go about her work. What a novel approach. In might not work, but she had nothing to lose. This party was important to her.

She walked to the door, surprised to see it was still in one piece. In the midst of the pounding she stood up straight, brushed back her hair with her fingers and put on a polite smile. Then her slightly shaking hand turned the handle and opened the door.

Ah, Mr. Depression and Mrs. Anxiety, how, uh. . . interesting to see you. Won't you please come in."

Thank you," said Mr. Depression in a slow, deep voice. "What an unfortunate day for a party. Looks like rain. Are you having to do all the preparations alone? How sad nobody cares enough to help you."

 Good afternoon," said Mrs. Anxiety in a rather tense tone. "What will happen if the guests are all late? What if they don't arrive at all? What if they don't like the food and nobody talks to each other? Everybody might have a terrible time and you'll have a reputation for being the worst hostess in the state!"

"Please make yourselves comfortable," said Mrs. Davis. "I'm sorry to say that I have a dozen things to do and I can't really sit down and chat. But make yourselves at home and help yourselves to tea and pastries if you like." And without pausing or revealing her suspense, Mrs. Davis turned and quickly walked to the kitchen where she proceeded to unpack the china.

Well, Mr. Depression and Mrs. Anxiety were dumbfounded. How could they be treated so rudely? Where were her manners, anyway? It took them a minute to compose themselves before they marched into the kitchen. "Now see here," said Mr. Depression. "How dare you let us in and not attend to us. What are we supposed to do while you scurry around doing your chores? We'll have none of this. Now you make us some tea and sit down and chat until we're ready to leave."

"Please forgive me," said our hostess. But I have things to do. If I sit and chat with you I'll not get anything done and my party will be a failure. You may follow me around if you like; I can't stop you. But I now I realize that while I can't keep you from coming, I don't have to attend to you while you're here. I don't mean to be inhospitable. You may stay as long as you like and help yourself to the food in the refrigerator. The TV is down the hall and there are some new self help videotapes you might find interesting. Really, though, I'd better get back to work."

And so it was that Mr. Depression and Mrs. Anxiety occupied themselves for a few hours while Mrs. Davis finished preparing for the party and began welcoming her guests. Though the uninvited pair were frustrated at first, they soon found comfort from several of Mrs. Davis' guests who were willing to spend the entire party with them. Mr. Depression was quite honored that one man spent much of the evening talking about him. A young woman gave Mrs. Anxiety such devoted attention, that she noticed little of the evening's activities. Mrs. Davis' party was a smashing success, for most of the guests. As for Mrs. Davis, she was so busy attending to her guests that she hardly noticed her uninvited couple at all. When the party was over and all the guests had left, she noticed that Mr. Depression and Mrs. Anxiety were nowhere to be found. "I wonder if someone gave them a ride home," she thought.

Acceptance and Action

When my mind is agitated and upset, it is generally not possible to think myself into a different state of mind. This is an example of the mind trying to fix itself. The passage of time alone will often allow the mind to settle down somewhat. But rather than ruminate on a sofa, it is wiser to take some kind of constructive action. Don't think that you are running away from your feelings. *You can't run away from your feelings.* You can accept them and, like an unpleasant companion, take them along while you do what you need to do. As you become more skillful in accepting your feelings, you may find that they don't have the power over your life that you once thought they had. Freedom is not attained by dwelling in a constant state of happiness and serenity. Freedom is the ability to live your life fully and meaningfully regardless of the range of feelings which occupy your mind and heart at any given moment.

Let's review where we are at this point. We've discussed two important skills. The first is

Acceptance

Acceptance is particularly useful in the following situations:

Relationships – we learn to accept others as they are, instead of trying to change them

Feelings/Thoughts – we learn to accept our internal experience even when that experience is unpleasant or uncomfortable

External Circumstances – we learn to accept the circumstances of our lives that we cannot control or change

The second important skill is . . .

Co-existing With Unpleasant Feelings

This skill is most useful when we must either:

Take action . . . even though we don't feel like it and would prefer to do something else; or

Restrain ourselves from action . . . even though we feel the tug and pull of strong feelings and compelling thoughts.

PRACTICE

1. Eating the same breakfast

Create a menu for a standard breakfast and then eat the exact same breakfast each day for two weeks. Make sure you specify the exact quantity of each food. Notice how your feelings and thoughts shift periodically as you feel the desire for a second cup of coffee or think "I really don't want to eat a banana this morning." Coexist with whatever feelings and thoughts arise and maintain your breakfast routine.

2. Meditation

Meditate daily for one week, sitting quietly for 20 to 45 minutes while continuing to bring your attention back to your breath. As you notice thoughts, feelings or body sensations, simply accept them and bring your attention back to breathing.

3. Accept Your Reaction, Delay Your Response

We often face provocative situations in life which stimulate an internal response (feelings/thoughts). Then we respond (behavior) immediately. This can be useful when we are facing an emergency, but in other situations we can learn coexistence with our feelings by accepting our reaction and delaying our response. An example of a triggering event might be critical comments by your mother-in-law or a poor report card from your teenage son. The next time you are faced with such a situation, try noticing and accepting your internal reaction, without responding for at least one hour. See if you can just "be with" your feelings of anger, tension, frustration, or similar feelings without saying or doing anything in response. During the hour, invite your feelings/thoughts to accompany you while you attend to other responsibilities. See what happens.

Resources

Krech, Gregg and Krech, Linda Anderson. *A Finger Pointing to the Moon*. Middlebury, Vermont: ToDo Institute, 1996, 2007.

Kora, M.D., Takehisa. *How To Live Well: Secrets of Using Neurosis*. Albany: SUNY Press, 1995

Maurer, Robert. *One Small Step Can Change Your Life: The Kaizen Way*. New York: Workman Publishing, 2004.

Reynolds, David K. *Constructive Living*. Honolulu: University of Hawaii Press, 1984

Skill #3

WORKING WITH YOUR ATTENTION

"I sometimes imagine that if the creator of the universe wanted to take another shot at communicating what was most important, she might replace all of sacred scripture with the words 'Pay Attention!' To choose the world means first of all to see it clearly, to shed fantasy and habit, to look, and look again, to let ourselves be broken open by its intricacy and its mystery."

- Philip Simmons (from Learning to Fall)

L ast night, the stars put me in my place, just as they have many times in the past. As I wandered down the hillside beyond my home I was accompanied by an old dog and a chatty, scattered mind. Then I looked up. As soon as I became aware of how big the universe is I realized how small I am. There were hundreds of glistening stars putting on a show entitled, "You (that's me) are not the center of the universe." Now this is not new information to me. I once asked a former teacher to review a draft manuscript and he commented on how many times I used the word "I" in my writing. The other day I was driving home behind a red Plymouth driven by an older woman with grey hair. Just when we reached the Y in the road before the general store, she went left as I took the road to the right. It suddenly dawned on me that this woman had an entire life that would be continuing at the same time as mine. She had problems, she had aches and pains, she laughed at jokes I had never heard before. How was this possible? Even more outrageous was the fact that there were about six billion other people who also had lives of their own. Incredible. My life was only a speck in a rather large crowd. There were also animals, and insects, and trees, and flowers, and buildings. This is what we might call perspective -- realistic perspective. And if my attention was reality-based it would reflect such a perspective. But it doesn't.

When we begin to seriously study attention, one of the first things we discover is how often our attention is focused on ourselves. Now we're feeling hungry. Now thirsty. Now we're worried about what's going to happen. Now we're tired. Now we're looking around the room, not thinking of others, but thinking, "I wonder what they think of me." We notice an item in a store and our reference point is "I could really use one of those." We call a business associate to meet for lunch and our primary concern is, "what's most convenient for me." In a recent winter storm 1,000 cattle froze to death, huddling together in an open meadow in a failed attempt to keep warm. When a reporter interviewed the rancher, his first comments were, "We're broke." My needs. My wants. My suffering. It's enough to make you sick. In fact, it does make you sick.

In 1990, psychologist Rick Ingram reviewed the research that had been done on the subject of self-focused attention. (Psych Bulletin, Vol. 107, No.2). This research covered problem areas such as depression, anxiety, alcohol abuse, and even schizophrenia. In each case there was an indication of a direct relationship between self-focused attention and the psychological problem. *"The weight of available data clearly suggests an association between disorder (or vulnerability to disorder) and self-focused attention regardless of the particular disorder,"* stated Ingram. Other researchers have drawn similar conclusions. A 1982 study of depression by Jacobson and Anderson found that *"depressed people refer to themselves more frequently than do nondepressed people, even when the normal flow of conversation calls for more attention to the other person."* (Behavior Therapy, Vol.13). They went on to conclude that ". . . *evidence also seems to suggest that happiness is associated with an outward focus."* Here we have one of the most fundamental and overlooked distinctions in the field of mental health -- the contrast between outward attention to the world and attention focused on ourselves. This distinction is a watershed between good and poor mental health, between a healthy, flowing mind and a suffering, self-absorbed one.

Paying attention, whether self-focused or outward, is a skill. We develop it in the same way we learn to play the piano. If we practice consistently with the left hand, we become good at playing with our left hand. If we practice with the right, we become good at playing with the right. A good pianist plays well with both hands. But I have much more dexterity with my right hand than my left. And I am sorry to report that I have much more dexterity attending to myself than to the world around me. I often daydream, plan, worry or do almost anything other than pay attention to what is going on around me at any given moment.

Nearly all of my students echo this self-diagnosis. We are not out of touch with our inner world, that world of feelings, of preferences, of desires and discomfort. It is a world we know too well. It is a prison which blinds us to a universe of sunsets, spider webs, and stars. A universe which is vibrant and breathing with life. The universe wants us to dance, but we are too self-absorbed to hear the invitation.

But not all the time. Every once in a while the beauty of the world around us is so stunning, so captivating that we can no longer ignore it and we forget ourselves and dissolve into something greater. And it is not only beauty which attracts us, it is also need. The need of a loved one for help, the needs of a community, even a planet. We find our calling, our bliss, our purpose, by giving up on ourselves. Our surrender becomes our salvation. Our disappearance provides relief, even for a few moments. But once you've tasted those moments you've discovered something about attention. And now you can travel through the world and seek out what isn't so obvious. The shadows of birches late in the afternoon. A weed growing in the fissure of a large boulder. The texture of a rose petal against your cheek. You're on your way to becoming a poet.

But the field of psychology is still preoccupied with self-preoccupation. Too often it teaches us to do what we already do too well -- pay attention to ourselves. In the course of exploring our pain, our worries, our feelings, and our dreams we forego the development of a more needed skill -- to notice and engage in the world around us. Without practice, these muscles atrophy. So the next time you find yourself self-absorbed, take a walk. Look around you. The world is an interesting place. It might even give you something to do. If the stars are out, close your eyes. Listen. You might just hear them twinkle. That is how they get your attention.

Past, Present and Future

The first "dimension" of attention is direction. We can direct
our attention inward or outward. Now let us consider the
second dimension of attention -- time. There are situations
where we want to place our attention on the past (self-
reflection) and also situations where we want to place our
attention on the future (planning). But most of the time it's
best to keep our attention focused on the reality of the present.
The present moment is the only reality available to us. We
can't really focus our attention on the past or the future, just
thoughts about the past and future. But in the present, we can
really pay attention to a sunset, cooking soup or playing with a
child. So the only way to be connected with the world in a
direct/sensory way is to repeatedly bring our attention back to
the present. With attention training you can improve your
ability to do this.

The key to staying present is to practice staying present. We
do this by noticing that our attention has drifted away from the
present and then we gently bring it back. For example, let's
say you're out of bed and have just started to take your
shower. As you're showering and washing your hair, your
mind is already planning the day's agenda. "Don't forget you
have that meeting a 9am." "Make sure you call your daughter
to find out how she did on the exam yesterday." "Hopefully
the check you wrote yesterday won't bounce before you get
that deposit to the bank today." Many of these kinds of
thoughts are about the future, and at least some of them
stimulate feelings of anxiety. "What if the check does
bounce?" So now you are anxious about events that haven't
even happened and may never happen at all. Rather than try to
"fix" your thoughts or feelings, all you need to do is bring your
attention back to the reality of your surroundings. Notice the
details of the showerhead (sometimes I'll count the number of
streams of water coming out). Feel the wetness of the water

streaming down your body. Notice the steam around you. Or the texture of the bathtub against the bottom of your feet. Listen, really listen, to the sound of the water as it forces its way through the showerhead. Now you are present. This is your real life -- the only true moment of life available to you.

Perhaps it seems boring. Perhaps you're so used to being entertained by your mind, that real life doesn't seem very interesting any more. That can happen when our attention becomes habitually focused on what's going on in our mind instead of what's going on in the world. Fortunately, there's an antidote to this problem – start paying attention to the world . . . *in detail*. Details make life interesting. Ask someone who is fascinated by carpentry, birds, golf, gardening, cooking, or just about anything and chances are they will passionately describe *the details* of their pursuit. When we start paying attention to details, life can become addictively interesting. And every time we notice the caw of a crow, or the scent of a lilac or the color of the sky at sunset we are coming back to the present. At first, this requires conscious effort on your part. But as you practice more and more, you will find that it starts to happen naturally. You start falling in love with life itself.

Because the eye loves novelty and can get used to almost any scene, even one of horror, much of life can drift into the vague background of our attention. How easy it is to overlook the furry yellow comb inside the throat of an iris, or the tiny fangs of a staple, or the red forked tongue of a garter snake, or the way intense sorrow makes people bend their bodies as if they were blowing in a high wind. Both science and art have a habit of waking us up, turning on all the lights, grabbing us by the collar and saying "Would you please pay attention!"

*- Diane Ackerman (**A Natural History of the Senses**)*

PING PONG OF THE MIND

My colleague, Margaret McKenzie, once wrote . . .

"I noticed my desire to have things be different and just kept returning to things as they are."

There is an ocean of wisdom in this single line. If we could just do this skillfully, how much of our suffering would simply dissipate. I wrote an essay on gratitude a while back that started by suggesting, "there is always something we can complain about." In nearly every situation, we can find something we're not happy about. Something we're not comfortable with. And then our attention gravitates to that element of reality. The sequence is often something like this:

1.   We attend to some element of our circumstances.

2.   We attend to our response (unpleasant feelings and/or thoughts) about that element of our situation.

3.   Our attention goes back and forth between #1 and #2 like a ping pong game.

4.   We attend to our thoughts about how the element of the situation should be different and how much better off we would be if it were different.

5.   Our attention goes back and forth between #1 and #2 and #4.

That ping pong game can go on for a long time. For the entire plane ride. For the entire party. For the duration of our relationship with X over 24 years! But when we just return to things as they are, we find that the single ping pong game is just one small element of the circumstances of our life. What else is going on? We have a cushioned seat. We are safe. There are birds chirping. There's a bathroom. We have unlimited access to drinking water. We have eyeglasses to help us see more clearly.

There is more going on in our life than this little ping pong game we've been playing. You can stop the ping pong game in a variety of ways, but it requires a shift of attention. You shift your attention away from #1 (that particular element of the situation). You shift your attention away from #2 (your thoughts and feelings). You shift your attention away from your ideas of how things should be different (#3 -- again, your own thoughts and feelings). Once the game stops, a whole new world appears!

Morita therapy has a name for the ping pong game – it's called *toraware* – the endless cycle of getting caught up in our self-focused thoughts. The other method of Japanese psychology, *Naikan*, also works with our attention by asking us self-reflection questions which naturally shift our attention. Both methods of Japanese Psychology make attention the central theme of the problem (our suffering) as well as the solution.

I was in China several years ago, visiting the orphanage where my oldest daughter spent the first ten months of her life. The same man, Mr. Cao, was still the director. I played ping pong with him. He's actually a very good player. I enjoyed playing for a few minutes. But I don't really want to play ping pong all the time. There's so much to do and see in the world. So after a while we stopped playing ping pong and went to the dining room where we had a wonderful meal of traditional Chinese food. The food was delicious. It was a feast worthy of my full attention!

THE NEXT STEP

On a hot summer day, my family and I climbed Azure Mountain in the Adirondacks and my body and mind got a great workout. My body worked hard to get to the top, particularly since I'm carrying a few added pounds these days. My mind got an equally good workout going down. The trail was narrow, wet and steep with an endless collection of exposed tree roots and slippery rocks peeking through the trail like hidden landmines. Thirty years ago I had surgery on my right knee, so climbing down becomes an exercise in focused attention. I have to be meticulous about where I place my right foot -- one misstep and that aging ligament replacement may snap and land me in surgery. So with the aid of a gnarled walking stick, generously supplied by my youngest daughter Abbie, I carefully and tediously picked my way down this treacherous trail, step by step. Rarely am I required to keep my attention so focused with such intense concentration. Periodically I would watch my attention turn inward with thoughts such as, *"There's no way I'm going to get to the parking lot without falling and twisting my knee."* My practice was to notice the shift of attention and move my attentional focus back to the present moment – which generally meant to the next step down the trail.

As I got close to the trailhead at the bottom, the trail widened and become relatively flat. The wet tree roots and slippery rocks were generally replaced by a soft bed of brown pine needles that gently cushioned the soles of my feet. My wife had waited for me and we walked the last five minutes together, side by side, chatting about the climb, the view and the kids. Gone was my meticulous attention to the next step. Gone was my immersion in the present moment. The comfort, safety and ease of the trail meant that I could become lazy. But the steep section of the trail, and my need to control and redirect my attention, resulted in a change in my brain, at least if you believe the current studies of what is now called neuroplasticity.

Neuroplasticity means that your brain is actually modified and resculpted, based on your behavior and what you pay attention to. In the words of researcher, Douglas Gentile, "The brain becomes what the brain does."

For people interested in psychology, mindfulness, Eastern philosophy and the brain, this is a fascinating time. First, we're seeing a widespread effort to integrate Buddhist ideas about the mind into counseling and psychotherapy. And second, we're seeing the emergence of a new generation of neuroscientists who are discovering that the brain is not hardwired, as had been thought. The brain actually changes in response to how we pay attention and what we pay attention to.

Suppose you go for a walk in your neighborhood and notice a beautifully restored 1950's sports car parked in the driveway of one of your neighbor's homes. You notice the car, because it's a new addition to your walk and its lines and shapes make it stand out amongst the other vehicles. Your attention has been "caught" by this car. This is what happens to us throughout much of our daily comings and goings. We notice a car, an unusual bird, a new billboard, a song in the background or even an aroma as we walk into the bakery. The objects of our attention are capturing our attention.

Our attention is also captured by our internal experience. We notice that we're feeling depressed or angry. We get caught by an ever-unfolding series of thoughts about the problems in our relationship with our partner. We ruminate.

This type of attention (passive attention) does little to improve our attention skills. To improve our attention skills, we have to take the lead on where we put our attention. We have to start directing and redirecting our attention. This is very exciting, because we are now asserting some control over a skill that is at the very heart of our experience of life itself.

Attention is a central element in so many important areas of your life like relationships, competence at work, gratitude, safety, memory, creativity and even spirituality. When we begin to study and practice attention we begin to see that we usually exert very little control over our attention and, ironically, it's the awareness of that fact that becomes the jumping off point for beginning to develop our ability to work with our attention skillfully.

Now there's only one way to develop a more skillful approach to your attention – Practice! You can't learn to play the piano unless you practice. You can't learn to ice skate unless you practice. And you can't improve your attention unless you practice. The most straightforward approach to attention practice is daily exercises. At the end of this chapter I've listed some sample exercises that you can use as you begin working to develop your attention skills.

MAXIMS

I'd like to offer you to two maxims that can help you as you work with your attention. The first is . . .

Your experience of life is not based on your life, but on what you pay attention to.

The river of life has a rich and dynamic current. There is infinite amount of activity going on in and around you all the time. Meteors are crashing into the earth's atmosphere and, at the same moment, a hair just fell off your head and onto the sofa where you're sitting. This happened while you were sipping a hot cup of tea as your dog lay sleeping and breathing rhythmically a few feet away. But what are you paying attention to? That is your experience of life. Are you noticing the flavor of the hot tea as it passes over your taste buds, or are you noticing the thoughts of the person who hassled you at work yesterday?

Do you know that most of our suffering doesn't exist in the present moment? There are times when we have a toothache or we fall off our bicycle. But much of our suffering comes from anxiety about the future (*What if I get mugged on my way home from the restaurant?*) or rumination about the past (*I'm so angry at him for making that rude comment about me*).

Two people could (theoretically) have the exact same events and circumstances occur throughout the day and one could go to sleep feeling depressed or frustrated, bemoaning what a rotten day it was, while the other falls to sleep feeling thankful for all the ways they were supported and cared for during the day. The circumstances are the same, but what they paid attention to was very different.

The second maxim I'd like to offer you is . . .

What you pay attention to grows.

Your attention is the equivalent of fertilizer for a plant. If you pay attention to the aches and pains of your body a lot, they grow in relative prominence to the rest of your life. If you pay attention to all the little services your partner does to take care of the home and family, they grow in your perception of that person. When I work with married couples who are in conflict, one of the first things I do is call a moratorium on problem solving. Usually the couple has spent an incredible amount of energy focusing on "the problem" that has stimulated so much tension or hostility between them. This problem is now the centerpiece of their marriage. Their attention keeps coming back to "the problem." So the best place to begin is to shift their attention. What is your wife doing for the kids that makes your life easier? What is your husband doing around the home that makes the home a nicer place to live? How can you surprise your partner today? How can you support your partner today?

In business and parenting you often hear advice that suggests we should "catch people doing something right." Our tendency is to notice when people make mistakes. We notice the mistakes and we point them out. Not only does this become our dominant line of communication – it becomes our habitual way of paying attention. So "mistakes" grow. We are fertilizing them. My daughter's piano teacher, Jody, does the opposite. When my kids are having a lesson, and they play a composition for her, she almost always begins her response by communicating something they did well. "Your timing was excellent." "You played the second arpeggio so smoothly." "You did a great job of playing that difficult part at the end of the second page." Of course, she also offers constructive feedback and direction. That's an important part of teaching. But by noticing what the student is doing right, she is nurturing those aspects of the child's capability. Not only is her attention on what the child did correctly, but she is shifting the child's attention to what they are doing well, which is encouraging and inspiring to the child's efforts to learn.

Keep these two simple maxims in mind. They provide great guidance when we are facing challenging situations that stretch us and force us to work at our edge.

DRIFTING ATTENTION

If you watch the clouds on a windy day, you'll notice them drifting across the sky. Our attention drifts as well. In this diagram you can see how attention drifts from one direction to another. To counter this "breeze" we have to be willing to periodically redirect our attention. This involves learning how to consciously direct our attention rather than just letting it drift aimlessly.

Attention Drifts

- My Feelings & Thoughts
- Sensations in My Body
- My Needs & Desires
- The Past
- The Future
- My Problems
- What Others Should Be Doing

- The Present Moment
- What I Am Doing
- The World Around Me
- How I Am Supported

Shifting our attention, from self-focused to outward-focused, depends a lot on the mental state we are in at any given moment. If we're highly emotional or in physical pain, for example, that shift becomes difficult. Actually what's difficult is that we keep getting pulled right back into focusing on our feelings or the pain in our body. Activities with specific characteristics can help us shift our attention more successfully.

The best chance we have of shifting our attention away from ourselves is when the activity:

1. *involves large muscle movement;*

2. *is fast-paced (rather than slow);*

3. *is unpredictable (rather than predictable);*

4. *involves engagement with others (rather than being alone).*

Examples of activities that are most likely to help us shift our attention include dancing, basketball, yard work, chopping wood, skiing, and mountain biking. Such activities are ideal, but often any kind of physical activity, like cleaning the garage or gardening can be helpful. The key is to get your body moving. Remember . . . lead with the body!

MISDIRECTED ATTENTION

In the following story, Shelly's attention is mostly self-focused. This kind of misdirected attention has many pitfalls. As you observe Shelly's experience, can you identify the price she pays for her unskillful attention. Can you identify the "costs" of misdirected attention?

Shelly noticed an old note on her desk from Marla asking her if she would be interested in joining a bowling team. She shrugged and thought, "Bowling -- how incredibly boring!" Shelly was still upset over Larry's comments at the meeting that morning. She had been caught off guard and had no idea he had such serious concerns. Why didn't he talk to her privately about these issues instead of raising them in front of the entire team? As she continued to replay the meeting over and over again in her mind she noticed the clock on her paneled wall. It was already noon. NOON! She had an appointment to meet Dave, her fiancé, for lunch at noon. Now she'd be at least 15 minutes late. She quickly closed down her computer, forgetting to save the report she was working on.

Shelly jumped into the elevator and pressed the button for the first floor. Dave had hesitated when she asked him to meet her for lunch because of a project which he was trying to finish at work. Now she would be late and he would be waiting. He'd probably be angry. Or maybe not. Maybe he would be late too and he wouldn't even realize that she was late. While her mind played with the possibilities, her opportunity to get off at the first floor had passed and she found herself on the ground floor instead. Now she would have to walk up a flight of steps and would be even later for her lunch date.

As soon as Shelly left the building she noticed the chill in the air. "Oh, why didn't I bring my sweater," she thought. Earlier that day she noticed a little tickle in her throat and a heaviness in her legs. She wondered whether she might be coming down with some kind of virus. Or perhaps it was something more serious. Last week she had noticed some unusual discomfort in her knees. Arthritis? Lupus? The possibilities were not pleasant. As she pondered them, she was startled by a screeching of brakes and noticed a blue Camaro that had screeched to a stop only a few feet to her left while she was crossing Delancy Blvd. The driver stuck his head out the window and yelled, "Why don't you watch where you're going?" As she quickly made her way through the intersection she thought, "Stupid idiot. What happened to the days when pedestrians had the right of way?"

She arrived at the restaurant at 12:20. A young man on his way out opened the door for her, but she was too flustered to even notice him. She heard a familiar voice, "Shelly, Shelly, over here." It was Dave. She had walked right past him when she entered the dining room. He stood up and they gave each other a warm embrace. "Oh, I've had such an upsetting morning. You wouldn't believe what happened," she said. And as they sat down she proceeded to describe the events of that morning, including her close call on Delancy Street. Though she had ordered her favorite entree, pasta primavera, she hardly noticed what she was eating as her attention danced between the morning meeting and what she needed to do that afternoon.

Dave looked at his watch and announced that he needed to rush back for a 1 pm meeting. "Why don't you run along," said Shelly. "Lunch is on me." Dave thanked her, grabbed his briefcase and hurried off. Shelly sat down, feeling somewhat disappointed that their time together was so brief. She glanced at the check and opened her purse to get a credit card. But to her surprise her wallet wasn't there. "Oh, no," she thought as her stomach twisted. "Where did I put my wallet?" She tried to remember the last time she had it. "Did I take it to work this morning?" "Did I stick it in my desk drawer?" A bus boy cleared the dirty dishes from her table and refilled her coffee cup. Alas, she didn't notice.

COSTS OF MISDIRECTED ATTENTION

1. Psychological Suffering

The more self-focused our attention is, the more we struggle with problems such as depression, anxiety, shyness, etc . . .

2. Making Mistakes

If we don't pay attention to what we're doing, we're bound to make more mistakes.

3. Safety Risks

Car accidents, muggings, accidents around the house . . . many injuries involve an element of unskillful attention.

4. Oversensitivity to Changes in the Body

Our bodies are constantly changing. If we pay too much attention to small or subtle changes, we become overly concerned that every change is a problem or serious illness.

5. Lack of Appreciation

How can we notice what others are doing to support us when our attention is constantly turned inward?

6. Boredom/Lack of Interest

When we pay attention to details, the world becomes interesting. When we're bored, we're usually not paying attention to details.

7. Not Noticing What Needs Doing

There is a world of difference between "doing what you feel like doing" and "doing what needs to be done."

8. Forgetfulness

Where was your attention when you put down your keys?

9. Wasting Time

How often do we waste time because of misdirected attention?

10. Causing Unnecessary Trouble to Others

Your life is not an island. The cost of your misdirected attention is often passed on to others.

CONCLUSION

Can you see how the skillful use of our attention is such a fundamental aspect of our life experience and how the unskillful use of attention often results in suffering? The challenge we face is to try to understand how our attention works and then improve our own attention skills. This is not an easy task. But with commitment, persistence and practice you can make significant changes in the way you use your attention. You can improve your concentration, your mental health, your intimate relationships, and your spiritual practice. What's at stake is nothing less than your experience of life itself.

Practice

1. Morning Mindfulness:

Set aside the first 30 minutes of each morning for one week as a mindfulness period. During this time, pay attention to the details of what you do from the time you get out of bed. Which foot touches the ground first? How many steps between your bed and the bathroom? What color is the cap on the toothpaste? How many times does your toothbrush go up and down when you brush your teeth? As your mind wanders and gets distracted, gently bring it back to the present moment. Each day try to notice details you may have missed the day before.

2. Get the Blues

Keep an eye open for the color blue today. **Whenever you remember ... look up (or down or out) and scan for blue,** from the smallest detail on your tea cup to the broadest of blue skies. Look for the breadth and the depth of blue. Different blues have different hues. Find vibrant blue, sweet blue, true blue, troubled blue . . . find your favorite blue. Discover blue treasures wherever they live today. When your attention is wandering uncontrollably, rein it in with the color blue.

3. Working with Your Attention Distance Learning Program.
Each April/May the ToDo Institute sponsors a month-long program on working with your attention. The program uses exercises adapted from Morita Therapy and Naikan-related approaches. Each day of the month offers an attention-related exercise. There is an audio program, course website and an advisor is available for questions.

Resources

Elkins, James. *How to Use Your Eyes*. New York : Routledge, 2000.

Nhat Hanh, Thich. *The Miracle of Mindfulness*. Boston: Beacon Press, 1976.

Krech, Gregg. *Life is a Matter of Attention* (audio program). Middlebury, Vermont: ToDo Institute, 2008.

Gallagher, Winifred. *Rapt: Attention and the Focused Life*. Penguin Press, 2009.

Skill #4

SELF-REFLECTION

"Sometimes I go

about in pity for myself,

and all the while

a great wind is bearing me

across the sky"

- Ojibwa (Native American) saying

There is an old prank where someone places a sign or sticker on the back of another person's coat or shirt. The sticker says something that is meant to be humorous, like "kick me." The person with the sticker walks down the street, around the office, in and out of restaurants or post offices and everyone else sees the sticker except the person wearing it.

I think most of us are the subject of this joke more than we realize. Each day we live our lives, conducting our business and personal affairs, and we seldom see ourselves the way others see us. Perhaps we frequently interrupt people when they speak, or we speak mostly about ourselves. Perhaps we eat very fast, or avoid taking responsibility for our mistakes. Maybe we get very defensive when anyone tries to give us advice, or are consistently late for meetings and appointments.

The image we have of ourselves is rarely the image others have of us.

This is not surprising for two reasons. First, we generally try to create a favorable image for others -- attempting to show only the wise, kind and admirable aspects of our lives and concealing the foolish or hurtful things that we do. But this strategy can never be completely successful. People begin to see through this public facade, particularly as they get to know us better. It is like the person who wants to be viewed as a meticulous housekeeper. Every time guests are expected this person takes all the clutter and throws it in the closets and the bedroom. When company arrives, everything looks very tidy, but the host must always be concerned that someone will accidentally open the closet or bedroom door and see a tremendous mess. Or perhaps someone will show up unexpectedly.

Secondly, we rarely take time to reflect on how we are living and how our conduct affects others. We may take time to exercise, watch TV, or talk on the phone, but we don't think of time for self-reflection as important or urgent. We don't think of it as a skill. Most of us would acknowledge that it is important to make time in our lives for quiet reflection, but then we get caught up in other activities. Self-reflection can open our eyes to the true nature of our life psychologically, spiritually and practically, as we consider our relationships with others.

The skill of self-reflection has three main components: the awareness of how I am supported by others, the awareness of the balance (or imbalance) between my giving and receiving, and the awareness of how I impact on the world around me.

Noticing the Support I am Receiving

The other day I had to drive to a restaurant in the city of Ottawa, Canada. I am not very familiar with Ottawa. I was able to find my destination, in part, thanks to the efforts of those who put up street signs and highway signs along the way. That took a lot of effort, time and money. Without such signs I would surely have been lost. Too often, I benefit from street signs without considering the efforts of those who put them up. But if there is a sign missing, or there is a conspicuous absence of proper signs, I will most surely take notice and complain, at least to myself. It is common to notice such things only when they are missing or not functioning properly.

Too often we take the simplest things for granted. But what does it mean to take something for granted? It means that we are being supported by someone, or something, but are not aware of that support.

The flush toilet is a good example. Having a toilet which flushes adds great convenience to our lives. Our bodies process food and take what is needed. The rest is discarded from our bodies and much of it ends up in the toilet. All we have to do is push down a lever and it disappears and is replaced by clean water. This is really an extraordinary event when you think about it. The toilet is only one element of a very complicated and planned waste disposal system. Throughout most of human history there were no flush toilets. In many parts of the world there are still no flush toilets. Yet how often do we flush the toilet and think, "Wow -- this is great. I'm so glad to have a toilet like this around." And what happens if we have visitors and the toilet doesn't function properly. We may get very frustrated or upset. We may blame the toilet, or the plumber, or the last person who used the toilet. Now the toilet has our attention. Now we notice it, but only because it *isn't* supporting us. Most of us are very good at noticing the support we aren't getting. It is a skill many of us have mastered and practice often.

In order to notice how we are supported, we need to pause. Sometimes this pause occurs naturally when someone offers us a seat on the bus or opens the door for us. But if we are in a hurry, these gestures of kindness don't capture our attention any more than a toilet does. It is hard to be skillful at self-reflection when you're in a hurry.

If we take the time to reflect skillfully and sincerely, we are likely to experience life very differently. We may learn to appreciate things before they are broken and people before they are gone. To go through life complaining about how poorly we are treated is a tormented way to live.

"Expressing gratitude is transformative, just as transformative as expressing complaint. Imagine an experiment involving two people. One is asked to spend ten minutes each morning and evening expressing gratitude (there is always something to be grateful for), while the other is asked to spend the same amount of time practicing complaining (there is, after all, always something to complain about). One of the subjects is saying things like, "I hate my job, I can't stand this apartment. Why can't I make enough money? My spouse doesn't get along with me. That dog next door never stops barking and I just can't stand this neighborhood." The other is saying things like, "I'm really grateful for the opportunity to work; there are so many people these days who can't even find a job. And I'm sure grateful for my health. What a gorgeous day; I really like this fall breeze." They do this experiment for a year. Guaranteed, at the end of that year the person practicing complaining will have deeply reaffirmed all his negative stuff rather than having let it go, while the one practicing gratitude will be a very grateful person. What you practice is what you are; practice and the goal of practice are identical, cause and effect are one reality. Expressing gratitude can, indeed, change our way of seeing ourselves and the world."

- *John Daido Loori Roshi*

NOTICING THE BALANCE OF GIVING AND RECEIVING

If you have a checkbook, you get a statement each month listing the deposits and withdrawals, as well as your balance. Each month you can review your statement and see exactly where you stand. You may have a balance of available funds, or you may be overdrawn. Self-reflection gives you a similar opportunity to review your life and relationships with others. Have you given more than you received? Does the world (or this other person) owe you? Or are you in debt, having received more than you gave? Many people go through life with the attitude that the world owes them. I deserve a raise . . . I deserve a new car . . . I deserve a spouse who handles more of the responsibilities around here. Self-reflection allows you to examine your account. Should you put more energy into getting more from others? Or into giving more to others -- trying to repay your debt?

Personally, I always saw myself as a very giving person until I started to look more accurately and concretely at the give and take in my life. I discovered that I've received much more than I've given. When I'm aware of this (and sadly, I often forget) I'm more likely to respond differently in my encounters with others.

"In ordinary life

we hardly realize

that we receive a great deal more

than we give,

and that it is only with gratitude

that life becomes rich.

It is very easy to overestimate

the importance of our own achievements

in comparison

with what we owe others."

- Dietrich Bonhoeffer

NOTICING THE IMPACT I HAVE ON THE WORLD

The third component of self-awareness is awareness of the impact we are having on the world around us. Most of us are aware of what we do that benefits others. We have no problem noticing when we open a door for someone, or help them carry groceries. We may consciously pat ourselves on the back for taking the extra time to be helpful. But often we are blind to the ways in which we cause trouble, inconvenience or difficulty for others.

I was having dinner at a restaurant one evening. A large group was having dinner at a nearby table and one of the women got up to take a picture of her group. She stood up and walked back from the table but she could not get the entire group in the picture, so she walked behind another table, within a few inches of the people eating dinner, and proceeded to focus her camera and orchestrate the picture. The people eating dinner at that table stopped eating and actually tried to get out of her way. After she snapped the picture, she returned to her seat without so much as apologizing to the couple for interrupting their dinner. I don't really think she had noticed that she almost sat in their pasta! She was so focused on focusing, that she was unaware that she was disturbing others. It is always easier to see this when someone else is the source of the inconvenience.

Once, on a flight to Hong Kong, I was eating dinner and having a very pleasant conversation about Japanese psychology with a nurse sitting next to me. The man in front of me had put his seat back, so I felt very cramped while trying to eat. As soon as I finished, I put my seat back to give myself some extra room. I was discussing how common it is to do things without being aware of the trouble we are causing others. I mentioned, as an example, putting one's seat back while the person behind you was still eating. Just at that moment, I glanced behind me and noticed a man, cramped behind my seat, trying to finish his meal. I had put my own seat back without even considering whether I was inconveniencing someone else, even as I was talking about this very idea!

Each day of my existence I cause troubles to other people and things. Sometimes I cause trouble with my speech (what I say to, or about, people. Sometimes I cause trouble with my driving, by creating air pollution or leaving my high-beam headlights on when another car is approaching. In the garden, I cause trouble by killing bugs and weeds. I cause trouble to people by being late for appointments or not returning calls or email promptly. I cause trouble to others by asking them to do things for me, or to my students by giving them assignments which are challenging and may stimulate unpleasant feelings. When I reflect on myself I have no trouble discovering ways that I have caused trouble -- though I am sure there are troubles I cause that remain hidden from my awareness. I simply do not see the situation from the other person's point of view. I do not have self-awareness, I am only thinking about myself. Thinking about myself and being self-aware are not the same thing.

To see a situation from another person's point of view is like magic. Mostly we see things only from a self-centered point of view. This means that when I consider a situation, I am considering my preferences, likes, dislikes, values, concerns, and welfare. But to see a situation from another person's point of view I must put myself in that person's shoes. This sounds easy, but actually it is quite difficult. How can I step outside of myself and understand what it is like to be another person? This is one of the challenges we must face if we are to reflect honestly on ourselves.

BENEFITS OF SELF-REFLECTION

Why is self-reflection important? Well, to begin with, self-reflection is one of the key ingredients of gratitude. The other key ingredient is attention. Attention and self-reflection provide the best conditions for us to cultivate an authentic sense of gratitude.

Over the years, we develop what I would call habits of attention. One of those habits is to frequently focus our attention on problems. If there's no particular problem at any given moment, your mind may ruminate about something that happened in the past or anticipate some difficulty that may occur in the future. It is common for our attention to focus on the problems and difficulties we are facing because we have to pay attention to such challenges in order to handle them. Unfortunately, we can develop a "habit of attention" in which we fail to notice the many things that are supporting our existence – our health, our work, our family, even people who provide public services like trash collection and keeping the electricity flowing. The more this "habit of attention" has developed, the less likely we will be able to experience gratitude.

I first made the connection between gratitude and attention when I discovered a Japanese method of self-reflection called Naikan (pronounced like the name of the camera). The word Naikan means "inside looking" or "inside observation." This method of self-reflection is primarily based on three questions:

1. What have I received from others?

2. What have I given to others?

3. What troubles and difficulties have I caused others?

As you can see, these questions are very simple. And when I participated in a 14 day retreat in Japan in 1989, these questions became the framework for me to reflect on my entire life. I reflected on each stage of my life and on every person who had playing a meaningful role since my birth (my mom, dad, grandparents, teachers, friends, colleagues, ex-girlfriends, etc. . .) When I stepped back from my life and began quietly reflecting on everything that had been done for me and given to me (question #1), I was surprised and overwhelmed by how much I had received in my life. The day I left that retreat I felt more cared for, loved and supported than ever before. It was as if I had a blood transfusion and gratitude was now simply flowing through my veins and arteries. I had learned to notice what I had not been noticing. Through self-reflection and shifting my attention I had developed a profound sense of gratitude for my life. I have yet to discover a more profound method for cultivating gratitude and reshaping our attitude and understanding of our lives.

"After the war, I went around telling people, "Thank you just for living, for being human." And to this day, the words that come most frequently from my lips are "Thank You." When a person doesn't have gratitude, something is missing in his or her humanity. A person can almost be defined by his or her attitude toward gratitude. For me, every hour is grace. And I feel gratitude in my heart each time I can meet someone and look at his or her smile."

- Elie Wiesel (holocaust survivor and recipient of the Nobel Peace Prize)

A second and important benefit of self-reflection is the impact it can have on our relationships with others. Even the wisest, most enlightened people can struggle with personal relationships. Self-reflection gives us a valuable opportunity to understand what it is like to be in the other person's shoes. We begin to get a glimpse of life from their perspective instead of our own. What is it like for my partner, or my colleague, to deal with someone like me? In this way, self-reflection opens up great possibilities for acceptance, understanding and conflict resolution in our most meaningful relationships. It shifts our attention away from blaming the other person to seeing our own responsibility for the situation. And it shifts our attention away from noticing how the other person is causing us trouble to how they are supporting us. Self-reflection is probably the single greatest tool we can use if we want to have successful relationships with others.

Finally, self-reflection, if it is done sincerely, makes us humble. Most of us judge the people around us. Sometimes we do this out loud, when we criticize someone who isn't present. But even if we don't speak about our judgments and criticisms, they appear regularly in our mental dialogue. We notice how others are messing up their lives – they're irresponsible, don't exercise enough, or are ignorant in their political views. They're not raising their kids properly, they're selfish, and lack compassion for others. The greatest antidote to our judgmental tendencies is to sincerely reflect on our own mistakes, transgressions and selfish behavior. As we remember these, our hearts have a tendency to soften and we are more likely to find compassion for the difficulties that others are experiencing, even if we consider them responsible for those difficulties.

Who and What Made It Possible for You to Be Here?

Do you recall those signs in the museums and zoos that say "You are Here"?

Well, right now you are somewhere, and I would like to offer you a short five minute exercise in reflecting on what made it possible for you to be there. Please take five minutes and reflect on this question?

Consider your parents and various ancestors – think about each one individually.

Think about where you are. Who else had a hand at helping you get there?

Think practically about objects. Were there objects that played an important role in making it possible for you to be there?

What about transportation?

What about other people beyond your parents and ancestors? Who else helped you to be where you are?

What about your education and skills? What do you need to know in order to be where you are? Who taught you?

Just investigate your life. Reflect and see what comes up for you?

If you spend even five minutes reflecting on this question you may be surprised at what you come up with. You may discover quite a rich supporting cast, ranging from parents to teachers to farmers and gas station attendants. When you bring this perspective into your awareness, notice how it affects your view of your life and yourself.

Self-reflection gives us an opportunity to see our lives from a very different perspective. It's difficult to gain this perspective as we go about our busy days trying to check off the items on our to-do lists. But it only takes a few minutes of self-reflection for us to see things quite differently.

A METHOD OF SELF-REFLECTION

When we think about self-reflection we may imagine going off to the mountains and taking time to just think about our life. But even when we find solitude in the mountains, or in a monastery, it is too easy to remain wrapped up in ourselves. Why did this happen to me? Why is my life so difficult? The kind of self-reflection I am referring to requires a redirection of our attention and a fundamental shift of perspective. There are several methods that are valuable. One of them is the moral inventory that is recommended in the 4th step of Alcoholic's Anonymous 12 step program. Another is the method used by Ben Franklin. Still another is reflection on the Buddhist precepts, known as *jujukinkai*. But the method I will discuss here is called **Naikan**.

Naikan was developed in Japan by Yoshimoto Ishin beginning in the 1940's and is used throughout Japan as a structure for people who wish to reflect honestly and sincerely on their lives. It has been applied to the fields of alcohol rehabilitation, clinical mental health, education, business and rehabilitation of criminals. But it is also used by ordinary people and by people who consider self-reflection to be an important element of their spiritual or religious practice. Naikan is one of the essential methods of the ToDo Institute's training and we have offered week-long Naikan retreats here for more than twenty years.

Let's look at the three Naikan questions I mentioned earlier, in the context of a relationship with another person.

The first question is:

What did I receive from _____?

The second question is:

What did I give to _____?

The third question is:

What troubles and difficulties did I cause _____?

Suppose you were to reflect on your relationship with your spouse. First you would choose a time period, perhaps the past month or past three months. Then you would begin to answer each of these questions, considering your relationship to your spouse during that time. Here are a few examples from my reflection on my wife, Linda:

What have I received from my wife?

She baked a special chocolate cake for me on my birthday. She watched our daughter for several hours every Sunday morning so I could play basketball or go for a bike ride. She sewed a button on my black pants. She balanced our checkbook at the end of the month. She washed my dirty clothes more than twenty times. She brought in some lilacs from the garden and put them in a vase in our bedroom.

As we list what we have received from the other person we're grounded in the simple reality of how we've been supported and cared for. In many cases we may be surprised at the length of the list and the importance many of the items play in our comfort and welfare.

And what did I give to my wife?

I gave her a back massage when she had a sore back. I bought her a book that she had been unable to find. I made travel arrangements so she could visit her mother. I bought and installed a new battery for her watch.

How does what I gave compare to what I received? When I look at the details, I get a better idea of the give and take in a relationship. Often we think the scales are tipped in our direction – perhaps they are. Or perhaps they're not. We're simply searching for the truth of the situation rather than holding on to our "story."

And finally, what troubles did I cause my wife?

I argued with her about putting in a door to the laundry room and delayed doing it for many weeks. I left it up to her to organize and manage all or our daughter's clothing. One evening she was very tired and I kept her up late talking about something that concerned me. I implied that she misplaced something of mine when, in fact, I had misplaced it.

The third question is the most difficult of all. To answer honestly, we have to be willing to see ourselves without the veil of defenses that often influence the way we perceive our relationships. We have to be willing to acknowledge our errors, transgressions, shortcomings and even our selfishness. Generally we think of this as a very unpleasant inquiry. We look at something that will probably make us feel bad or guilty? But an honest self-examination of our conduct is essential to our well-being, psychologically and spiritually. We can choose to avoid it, but it doesn't change the facts of how we've lived our life.

Of course there would be many more items on my list of answers for each question if I were to print everything I remembered. In general, you should reflect on another person for at least 45 to 60 minutes to make sure you have enough time to consider many different incidents and events. You should also make sure your answers are specific (she spent an hour editing my article) and not general (she was supportive and helpful). How did you know she was supportive? Think specifically about what the other person actually did, about what you actually did and about the specific trouble you caused. An example of Naikan reflection (daily Naikan) can be found at the end of this chapter.

Naikan helps you to see a more realistic picture of your life. Many of us do not see clearly because our interactions with others are often colored by our emotions. For example, if you get in an argument with your husband while he is driving you to the train station, what dominates your awareness – anger about the argument or appreciation for the ride? While the argument and the ride are both facts, the anger, with its emotional charge, may take center stage. It's difficult to feel grateful towards someone who just gave you a ride, if you are feeling very angry towards that person about something else. But the facts of the situation remain intact. Naikan can help ground you in your factual existence, which can give you a very different perspective on your life. A grateful perspective. A humbling perspective. A realistic perspective.

I have written in depth about the more profound aspects of self-reflection in my books on Naikan. These aspects relate to issues of faith, interdependence, human nature, and the fundamental purpose for which we exist. Naikan can give you some insight into these matters, if you are willing to investigate your life deeply and sincerely.

Examine life

outside

the boundaries

of

your suffering

- Gregg Krech

"Clinical studies show that gratefulness tends to build and strengthen social bonds and friendship, while narcissism impedes the feeling of gratitude. Not only are those who practice gratitude happier, they are also healthier, exercise more frequently, and are more apt to be helpful to others. Practicing gratitude does not buffer individuals from experiencing unpleasant emotions – but it may help people develop resources to successfully weather unpleasant emotional states."

- Robert Emmons and Joanna Hill (Words of Gratitude for Mind, Body and Soul)

OBSTACLES TO GRATITUDE

Because self-reflection and gratitude are closely related, let's consider three of the greatest obstacles to gratitude. They are:

Self-preoccupation

When we become preoccupied with our own thoughts, feelings, needs and body problems, we have little attention left over to notice what is being done to support us. You might think of your attention as a flashlight. As long as you shine the light on your problems, difficulties, and aches and pains, there is no light available for seeing what the world doing for you. If you don't notice how the world is supporting you, it's hard to be grateful.

Expectations

When I turn the switch on my bedside lamp, I assume the light
will go on, since it (almost) always does. Now that I've come
to expect this lamp to work, I hardly give it a thought. Once
I've come to expect something, it no longer grabs my attention.
But when the light doesn't go on – I take notice. So my
attention is automatically drawn toward that which is
unexpected. As a result, I'm more likely to notice those
aspects of my day where my expectations aren't met and
things don't go as planned. And I mostly ignore, and take for
granted, the smooth-running aspects of my day. This seems to
be our natural tendency.

Entitlement

I may recognize what I have been given. But the more I think
I've earned or deserved something, the less likely I am to feel
grateful for it. As long as I think I'm entitled to something I
won't consider it a gift. This sense of entitlement deprives us
of the joy and appreciation we might otherwise experience
when encountering the gifts and blessings of life.

To experience a sense of heartfelt gratitude we must overcome
these three obstacles. Self-reflection provides a path for doing
so. It allows us to pause to appreciate what is being given to us
rather than focus on what we don't have. It helps us to consider
the countless objects and human beings that made it possible
for us to get to work or turn on the computer. Through self-
reflection, we can look through eyes of humility and recognize
everything we have, and are, as gifts. And through self-
reflection we begin to train our attention to notice what we
haven't noticed.

Obstacles Along the Path

Years ago, on a lovely morning in April, I hiked up a trail towards a magnificent peak from which endless miles of Blue Ridge mountains and valleys could be viewed. The trail was rocky and ran along a creek, winding through a dense forest of pine, hemlock and maple. Storms from the winter season had left many trees and limbs across my path, creating unexpected detours. As I hiked up the trail, I found myself growing more and more agitated by the constant delays of coping with so much fallen timber.

After about three hours of hiking I reached my destination. The view surpassed my expectations and a crisp breeze swept up the valley walls. As I enjoyed the view, I recalled the difficulty involved in making my way past all of that fallen timber on the way up. One section of trail had resembled the hurdles event in the Olympics. Further up the trail I found a fallen tree with a double trunk, requiring a skillful slither above one trunk and below the other. How much easier my climb would have been had the fallen timber been cut away with a chain saw, leaving a pleasant, unobstructed path from beginning to end.

At that moment I vaguely recalled that some timber had, in fact, been cut away to clear the path. I remembered a few places in which a section of the trunk had been surgically removed, leaving the bottom and top of the tree resting unobtrusively on either side of the trail.

How interesting that I could so clearly remember trees that blocked my way, but only with the greatest effort could I recall that there were a few obstacles that had been removed.

As I made my descent I noticed quite a few of these "cut" trees and decided to do some research. For a fifteen minute period I counted both the trees that obstructed the path as well as those that had been cut to clear the way. The former were easy to count because they were in my way. If I didn't pay attention to them I'd trip over them. Noticing the latter, however, required additional concentration. I had to scan the borders of the trail for the cut ends of the logs.

At the end of the sample period I counted 42 obstacles. However, 47 trees had been cut to make the path easier! The reality was that more trees had been cleared than remained blocking the path. Yet during my ascent it was the obstacles that dominated my memory of the experience.

For many of us, this hike resembles our lives. We notice the obstacles because we have to get around them to proceed. But what if we go through life only noticing obstacles, problems and difficulties? Shouldn't we then expect our experience to be one of anger, hurt, disappointment and anxiety? Why not also notice the support, care and kindness we receive each day? Through such awareness, we discover the invisible gifts of life. Trees that have been cleared reappear as kindness. The efforts of farmers and supermarket clerks magically appear in the food we are served. The faces of our grade school teachers flow into the words we write.

Miracles are unnecessary, because even a telephone call, or a tomato are, by nature, miraculous.

Practice

1. Daily Naikan. For ten consecutive days spend 30 minutes each evening reflecting on your day (just the past 24 hours). Use the Naikan questions to review what you have received from others, what you have given and what troubles you have caused. Write your answers down in three separate columns. A sample of Daily Naikan can be found at the end of this chapter. Additional samples can be found on the ToDo Institute Web site:

http://www.todoinstitute.org/naikan4.html

2. Self-reflection Distance Learning Program. Each year the ToDo Institute sponsors a month-long program on self-reflection during November. The program uses exercises developed from Naikan as well as from other methods and traditions and provides you with a different self-reflection exercise each day of the month. An advisor is available for questions.

3. Naikan Retreat. Centers currently exist in Japan, U.S., Austria and Germany which allow people to engage in a one week intensive Naikan retreat. During this week you spend about 100 hours in quiet self-reflection reviewing your life and relationships with others. The Gregory Willms Memorial Naikan Fund provides no-interest loans to those who need financial assistance.

Resources

Krech, Gregg. *Like a Leaf on the Waves: Naikan and the Path of Pure Land Buddhism*. (unpubished manuscript)

Krech, Gregg. *Naikan: Gratitude, Grace and the Japanese Art of Self-Reflection*. Berkeley: Stone Bridge Press, 2002.

Steindl-Rast, David. **Gratefulness, the Heart of Prayer: An Approach to Life in Fullness**. Paulist Press, 1984.

Sample of Daily Naikan

What Did I Receive from Others?

Jody gave piano lessons to my daughters

My car got me back and forth to town without problems

Painted lane markers on the road made it easier for all the drivers to stay in their lanes.

Post office clerk gave me a money order

Bank clerk cashed a check for me

Linda made a delicious salad for dinner

Ruah made a homemade apple pie for dessert

Louis played the harmonica for us

Use of computer, electricity, phone lines, internet

Heat in the office

Sunny day warmed up the house

Working in an office with more windows than walls

Use of eyeglasses to see more clearly

The watch that Linda had given me years ago provided the time of day for me today

Hot water, soap, shampoo, towel for shower

Toothpaste and toothbrush for my teeth

Dishwasher washed nearly all the dirty dishes

Mary took mail to the post office

Granola, apple and juice for breakfast

Chani's singing in the car on the way home from piano lessons

My jacket kept me warm outside

Mary's help in office getting organized for beginning of Naikan program

Cup of coffee in the morning

Hugs from Chani after she opened birthday presents

Bob's tentative agreement to take care of Barley (our dog) while we're gone

Judith agreed to let Chani come visit the farm tomorrow (thank you, Judith)

What Did I Give to Others?

Several birthday presents to Chani

Got money order to send to Sasha who is sick overseas

Responded to numerous questions about the Naikan program from participants

Agreed to reschedule phone meeting for convenience of my assistant editor

Made a special breakfast for Chani for her birthday

Helped put together pizzas for dinner

Helped clean up after dinner

Stayed up late to wait for dishwasher to finish

Took girls to piano lessons

Lent two books and a DVD to Barbara

What Troubles and Difficulties Did I Cause Others

Haven't scheduled Spring Naikan retreat and people are waiting for a date.

Didn't give Jody a check for piano lessons (forgot checkbook)

Didn't buy mushrooms at store the day before so there were no mushrooms for pizza

Polluted air and contributed to global warming by driving about 45 miles in the car

Didn't send money order to Sasha yet, as promised

Interrupted Linda twice while she was working with Abbie on math homework

Talked on phone to Bob while Barbara was here after dinner

Left birdfeeder empty

Made Abbie go to bed even though she wanted to stay up later

Expressed frustration toward Linda when she arrived home later than expected

Forgot to send a birthday card or even email greeting to Steve

We imply, and often believe, that habitual vices are exceptional single acts, and make the opposite mistakes about our virtues -- like the bad tennis player who calls his normal form his bad days, and mistakes his rare successes for his normal.

-C.S. Lewis

Practice is Practicing

When I work with students individually, I often perform an assessment of the person based on these four skills:

1. Acceptance

2. Coexistence with Unpleasant Feelings

3. Paying Attention

4. Self-Reflection

The type of training, assignments and reading materials I offer is based on identifying the individual's weakest areas and systematically improving those areas through training and practice. When a person has identified a problem, such as depression, I also consider the relevancy of a particular skill to that problem. For example, depression tends to be more related to the first and third skills identified above, while relationship conflicts tend to be more related to acceptance and self-reflection. This is an assessment framework we use when we train counselors, therapists, teachers and coaches in our certification program.

We cannot think ourselves into being more skillful. Neither can we develop greater skill through philosophical commitment or intellectual understanding.

Skill development requires attention and action. It requires practice. The exercises described in each of the skill areas are a good place to start. Some of the books listed as resources provide additional exercises. If you wish to devote your life to self-development and learning, use each day to focus your energy on some type of practice. Through such effort we discover both competence and humility.

THE BODY'S INFLUENCE ON THE MIND

EXERCISE AND DIET

About 75 years ago, Japanese psychiatrist, Shoma Morita, M.D., suggested a rather radical idea -- that the body and mind were interwoven into the fabric of our being and that by using the body we could often have a dramatic effect on the mind. His notion of a body-mind connection, that the mind and body are one entity, has become a cornerstone of progressive medicine for the past thirty years, yet the emphasis is nearly always on the mind and its influence on the body. Robert Ader, Ph.D. of the Univ. of Rochester School of Medicine says, "I find it a little unbalanced that we talk more about how the mind can be taught to influence the body than about how the body can influence the mind." Morita's work is very much a study in how the body can influence the mind.

In its simplest form it is about taking appropriate action while learning to co-exist with a state of mind that attempts to hold us back. We go out jogging to get some exercise even though we feel lethargic and unmotivated. We return a phone call to a collection agency even though we feel tense and anxious as we're about to do so.

In each case the action itself is likely to influence our feelings and thoughts. Do what you need to do and let your feelings come along for the ride. Often the ride itself has a dramatic impact on your feelings.

What we put into our bodies also affects our minds. You may be familiar with the feelings of lethargy and sluggishness that surface after a big Thanksgiving dinner. Or the quick rise and subsequent crash of energy that comes from a candy bar. The consequences of diet go beyond the health of the body and extend their influence to the mind, as well.

So let us consider the two elements of mental wellness in which the body exerts its greatest influence on the mind: exercise (moving our bodies) and diet (feeding our bodies).

MOVING BODIES

"Endurance athletes, in particular, have reported that it is virtually impossible to train long and hard and be depressed. Because the athletes are concentrating on thoughts such as their training goals and the physical sensations of the workout, it is likely that their minds are taken off depressing and troubling thoughts."

- Larry Leith, Ph.D.

O n a chilly winter day in Vermont, the sound of a cherry log being split by an axe makes a "crack" that's clean, crisp, and immediate. The axe and its partner, gravity, do the bulk of the work and the log responds by revealing its inner beauty of smooth, reddish grain formerly sheltered by dark, nubby bark.

It's been more than two months since I split any wood. To be honest, the period from Thanksgiving to late January has been a rather sedentary one for me. Normally an active fellow, I feel like I have been hibernating with the bears. A combination of circumstances -- a newly adopted baby, the Christmas holidays, Vermont winter weather -- threw my exercise regimen into "park." I took a walk here and there and I still played basketball on Sundays. But by Thanksgiving, bike rides and hikes in the mountains had been replaced by diaper changes. The latter, while a great exercise in finger dexterity, appears to do little for the rest of my body. . . or my mind.

When we think of exercise, we often think of getting the body in shape. But personal experience and research in the field of exercise and mental health demonstrate that an active body is a key element of mental wellness. It can lift your mood, restore your spirit, combat depression, and relieve feelings of anxiety. It can help you shift your attention away from useless ruminations and toward the world around you. It can help relieve the stress of complicated and challenging situations. Bodies were designed to move and our minds were designed to inhabit moving bodies. By keeping your body active, you naturally nourish your mind.

The history of exercise and mental health goes as far back as Hippocrates, the father of medicine, who reportedly prescribed exercise for patients suffering from mental illness. But contemporary western psychology tends to neglect the natural treatment of body movement in favor of either talk or medication. Not surprisingly, a 1984 survey by Renee Royak-Schaler, Ph.D., found that the therapists who are most likely to prescribe exercise are those who exercise themselves. Still, for most counselors and consumers, exercise is an afterthought when it comes to mental health, rather than a serious aspect of the treatment plan. One holistic doctor we know actually writes a prescription for exercise and hands it to his patients – "30 minutes of exercise 3x/week".

Many of us are clear about the benefits of exercise to our bodies -- weight loss, lower blood pressure, reduced risk of heart disease, osteoporosis and breast cancer, as well as a stronger immune system. But can we take exercise seriously when it comes to mental wellness?

MOVING OUT OF THE BLUES

"Regular exercise may be the most powerful antidepressant available."

- Michael Murray, N.D.

Much of the research examining the relationship between exercise and mental health has occurred in the past 30 years. A great deal of that research focused on exercise as treatment and prevention of depression. One of the first major studies was by John Griest, M.D., in 1978. He found that exercise, by itself, was more effective in lowering symptoms among depressed patients than therapy. A more recent study in Norway (1989) surveyed 43 patients one to two years after being treated in a hospital for major depression. Each person was asked to evaluate the different types of therapy received while being treated. The range of therapies included antidepressant medication, community meetings, individual psychotherapy, group psychotherapy, contact with staff and other patients, and physical exercise. Overall, the respondents ranked physical exercise as the most important element of their treatment program. Other studies came to similar conclusions -- physical exercise produced either comparable or better results than many other forms of treatment for depression.

Exercise has not only been shown to be helpful in treating depression, but also helpful in preventing it. In one of the most recent population-based studies (Paffenbarger, Lee and Leung, 1994), researchers found that men who expended 1000 to 2500 calories per week in walking, stair climbing, and sportsplay were 17% less likely to develop symptoms of clinical depression than their less active peers. Furthermore, those who were most active, expending more than 2500 calories per week, were even less likely (28%) to develop clinical depression.

In 2001, Duke Univeristy researchers reported on their study of 156 older patients diagnosed with major depression. Researchers found that after 16 weeks, patients who exercised showed improvement comparable to those who took anti-depression medication. A follow-up study, which followed the same participants for an additional six months, found that patients who continued to exercise were much less likely to see their depression return than the other patients. Only 8 percent of patients in the exercise group had their depression return, while 38 percent of the drug-only group experienced relapse.

Numerous other studies document the beneficial effects of exercise in treating and even preventing depression, prompting psychiatry professor Jerry May, former chair of the U.S. Olympic Committee's Sports Psychology Committee to say, "Exercise is about as close to a panacea as you can get, and I don't believe in panaceas."

What Kind of Exercise is Best?

Intuitively you might think that the best type of exercise, particularly for depression, would be some type of high intensity aerobic exercise like running or basketball. It's only recently that researchers have begun to study and compare different types of exercise and the results are promising, particularly for those of us who are not aspiring to become professional athletes.

Surprisingly, most researchers have found little or no difference in the effects of aerobic versus non-aerobic exercise. When it comes to mental health, weight lifters (non-aerobic) appear to benefit as much as runners (aerobic). According to Larry Leith, professor at the University of Toronto and author of Exercising Your Way to Better Mental Health, "The exercises we have discussed appear to have two common elements. They involve the large muscle groups (arms, legs, and torso) and are rhythmic in nature. Any exercise that meets these two criteria will probably be effective in reducing depression."

How Long and How Often?

Whether you're planning on a refreshing walk to the grocery store, a yoga class, or weight lifting, experts recommend that you exercise at least three times per week for a minimum of 15 to 30 minutes per workout. Often a single workout will influence your state of mind, but it may take up to ten weeks to notice the effects of exercise on your overall state of mental health. Remember that you don't need "motivation" to get started, nor do you need to "feel like exercising" to get yourself to the gym or out for a run. Just use your behavior to influence your feelings. So go and work out, even when you don't feel like it, and notice whether your feelings change when you're passing the halfway point on your run or splitting your hundredth log.

The other day, after too many hours in front of books and a computer screen, I bundled up my daughter, strapped her into my kid-carrier backpack and walked down the driveway and up the road after a fresh snowfall. It wasn't until I had to climb the hill back up to the house that I began noticing the extra 20lbs. on my upper back. My pace slowed noticeably until I reached the back door where I was greeted by a warm fire. My daughter and I each got what we needed. I got some fresh air and a great walk which tired my muscles and woke up my mind. My daughter got a bumpy ride which put her to sleep. Time for a cup of tea while she dances in her dreams.

Practice

1. Distance Parking. When you park your car, at work or at a shopping center, park in the space that is furthest from the building to which you are going and walk.

2. Regular Exercise. Set up an exercise schedule for the next 30 days that involves at least 30 minutes of exercise 3 to 4 times per week. Stick to your schedule.

3. Cycling Errands. Get a bicycle (and helmet) and begin using it for short excursions or errands where you would normally take your car.

4. Dog Walking. Adopt a four-legged friend from your local animal shelter (or volunteer at the shelter) and notice how helpful it is when someone depends on you for their exercise.

Resources

Ratey, John J. **Spark: The Revolutionary New Science of Exercise and the Brain.** Little, Brown & Co, 2008

Leith, Larry. **Exercising Your Way to Better Mental Health**. Morgantown, WV: Fitness Information Technology, Inc., 1998.

Morgan, William, editor. **Physical Activity and Mental Health**. Washington, D.C.: Taylor and Francis, 1997.

Greist, J.H. **Exercise intervention with depressed outpatients.** In W.P. Morgan and S.E. Goldston (Eds.), Exercise and Mental Health. Washington DC: Hemisphere Publishers, 1987.

Food and Your Mind

"I don't talk to a patient

until we've spent some time on their diet."

- psychiatrist, Abram Hoffer, M.D.

Ralph stood a few feet from the heavy glass door and was careful to stay under the awning so he wouldn't get wet as the rain steadily fell. He still had about ten minutes before his appointment with his therapist, and he took advantage of the time to smoke a cigarette. He takes a similar smoking break about 40 times a day. About an hour ago he had lunch at McDonald's -- a Big Mac, large fries and a milk shake. He often has lunch there. It's cheap, quick, and convenient. Sometimes he eats dinner there as well. For breakfast, he'll stop at the bakery and get two donuts and a big mug of black coffee. He claims the coffee keeps him going. He grabs a cup whenever he has the chance.

Ralph is receiving counseling for his drinking -- alcohol, that is, not the coffee. He's been in counseling for ten years. He's also been in detox programs, rehab programs, and AA meetings. He's been on the wagon now for the past six months. Once he remained sober for an entire year.

There are certain things Ralph's counselor is interested in. She's interested in his self-esteem. She's interested in his childhood relationship to his parents. She's interested in his feelings of anxiety, his frustration and his anger at those who let him down. She's not interested in his diet. The only time she ever mentioned it was when she bumped into him at McDonald's during lunch and asked him how his lunch was. She's not interested in his exercise regimen and the fact that he's 50 pounds overweight. She's not interested in his smoking since he religiously abides by the office's NO SMOKING sign and always smokes outside. She's also interested in him showing up for his appointments on time and, of course, she's very interested in whether he's been drinking. What a counselor is interested in and not interested in is, well, interesting.

Inside the door of the clinic we find Lucy with her nine year old son Jake. Jake has been diagnosed with ADHD (Attention Deficit Hyperactivity Disorder). He's having problems at school. He has trouble concentrating and sitting still. His teacher describes his behavior as disruptive and sometimes aggressive. The psychiatrist at the clinic and the school social worker both suggest that he begin taking the medication Ritalin. They haven't given Lucy any other alternatives. What about Jake's diet? Could his problems be at least partly related to his high intake of sugar everyday? Or could he be allergic or sensitive to certain foods or food additives. Well, no one has discussed this possibility with Lucy. She has been assured, however, that her insurance will pay for Jake's medication.

There's one more person in the waiting room this morning -- Marcy. Marcy is depressed. She sits slumped in her chair, absorbed in thought and clutching a half-full can of Coke in her left hand. Marcy has been a regular client at this clinic for years now. Like Ralph, she is seriously overweight, though she doesn't smoke. Neither does she exercise or work. She's been on several different medications over the past five years. Nothing seems to really help. She stopped taking her medication once and was warned by her counselor that it was extremely important that she take her pills. She missed a session last month and never called. The staff made it clear, in a very polite way, that they expected her to call in advance if she needed to cancel. But there are no expectations of Marcy when it comes to her diet. She receives no advice or guidance. Diet and exercise are simply not part of "therapy" as most of us know it. But should they be?

WHAT WE PUT INTO THE BODY INFLUENCES THE MIND

A growing amount of literature and research suggests that food can have a dramatic effect on one's mood and even on clinical problems such as depression, panic attacks, alcoholism, anxiety, Alzheimer's, eating disorders and schizophrenia. Yet most of us aren't aware of the significant influence diet and nutrition can have on our thoughts, feelings, and behavior.

In 1968, Linus Pauling published a paper in Science magazine in which he introduced the term "Orthomolecular Psychiatry" and suggested that nutritional and vitamin deficiencies could be responsible for certain mental disorders. As a Nobel Prize winning chemist he spent years surveying and evaluating research and concluded that "nutrition should be a part of the treatment of every person with mental problems." His work drew attention from a small group of physicians and others at a time when the field of psychiatry was turning more and more to psychiatric medication and away from psychotherapy. Abram Hoffer, M.D., had begun working with schizophrenic patients in the 1950's and had a great deal of success in treating them with high doses of Niacin (Vitamin B3). He was intrigued by the similarity between the psychotic symptoms of schizophrenic patients and those with the medical disease pellagra. We now know that pellagra is a vitamin deficiency disease that can be cured by small amounts of Niacin. The discovery of a "cure" for pellagra and Hoffer's success with schizophrenic patients provided evidence that at least certain mental health problems can be associated with dietary and nutritional deficiencies.

Today there are a small but growing number of physicians who use nutritional strategies as a primary intervention for those with mental health problems. In the book, Nutritional Influences on Mental Illness: A Sourcebook for Clinical Research, Dr. Melvin Werbach, a professor at the UCLA School of Medicine, has attempted to create a comprehensive knowledge base of information on nutrition and mental health problems. The book covers twenty specific mental disorders ranging from anxiety to obsessive-compulsive disorder. Dr. Werbach states that:

"It is clear that nutrition can powerfully influence cognition, emotion and behavior. It is also clear that the effects of classical nutritional deficiency diseases upon mental function constitute only a small part of a rapidly expanding list of interfaces between nutrition and the mind."

We can consider the connection between diet and mental health as having four components:

1. Nutritional deficiencies. Inadequate amounts of particular vitamins or nutrients impact on the way the mind functions. This can be related to a wide variety of mental health problems.

2. Sugar metabolism. Blood sugar rises and falls in relation to sugar consumption. This affects our moods and energy levels and is a key element related to problems such as alcoholism and depression.

 3. Brain neurotransmitters. Different foods promote absorption and maintenance of different amino acids. For example, the amino acid tryptophan is used to make serotonin, the same neurotransmitter that is regulated by certain antidepressant medications.

4. Food allergies. Individual sensitivities to certain foods may trigger reactions internally (feelings/thoughts) and influence our behavior. This is a key element related to problems such as hyperactivity (ADD and ADHD) and anxiety.

Each of the above areas can be quite complex and I recommend that you do further reading to familiarize yourself with these issues in more detail. For now, let's take a closer look at the problem of depression and its relationship to diet and nutrition.

DEPRESSION AS A RESPONSE TO LIFE CIRCUMSTANCES

Let's take a look at depression, a mental health problem that affects more than 12 million individuals each year and causes suffering not only to the depressed person but impacts their families and workplaces as well. We mentioned Marcy earlier and stated that she has been struggling with depression for many years. Before we look further at her options we should distinguish between the kind of depression that is associated with some unpleasant or challenging life situation and the kind that is more pervasive and seems unrelated to the person's problems or difficulties. For example, people will often feel depressed after the death of a loved one or after losing their job. In such situations, it is less likely that diet is a major factor influencing feelings of depression. People may seek counseling at such times, but I find that eventual relief comes in four ways:

1. Time passes. Though feelings and thoughts may continue to arise, they are less intense and more bearable.

2. Acceptance. A spiritual or religious context, in which to see and understand reality, often provide a helpful basis for accepting what is out of our control. Eventually we must come to accept even that which is "unacceptable."

3. Constructive activity. Where there is action needed (such as looking for another job), constructive activity allows us to change our situation and also provides a healthy distraction from being absorbed in our own feelings and thoughts.

4. Self-reflection. Considering past events and relationships within the framework offered by Naikan can allow us to see the situation more clearly, stimulate appreciation, and promote responsibility for our own conduct.

NUTRITION AND DEPRESSION

"Nutrition is important in preventing depression and treating it. Often the quality of the diet suffers in depressed people. If the depression is profound, the individual doesn't even feel like eating . . . They're apt to restrict their nutrition to fast food or just anything to get eating over with."

- William Goldwag, M.D.

L et's assume there is no clear event or life situation that appears to have triggered Marcy's depression. If she were to look at the dietary or nutritional factors that might be playing a part in her depression, what would she find and what could she do?

First let's take a look at specific nutrients. The chart on page 109 indicates that deficiencies in B vitamins, particularly Vitamin B6 and B12 can be associated with depression. Another common vitamin deficiency in people who are depressed is Folic Acid. Research also shows that depression is a common clinical symptom of scurvy in humans, a disease caused by a deficiency in Vitamin C.

Now let's look at Marcy's diet. Marcy drinks 4 to 6 cans of Coke each day, often preceded by 2 to 3 cups of caffeinated coffee when she wakes up in the morning. The Coke gives her steady shots of caffeine and sugar, both of which can create chaos with Marcy's blood sugar and energy level and can be contributing significantly to her experience of depression. Her "sweet tooth" further adds to her sugar intake. From morning till night the frequent shots of sugar Marcy gets drive her blood sugar up and her body responds by releasing insulin to bring her blood sugar down. If Marcy is sugar sensitive or hypoglycemic, she craves a candy bar or cup of coffee as her blood sugar falls and the cycle starts once again. Marcy's body is taking her mind on a roller coaster ride – up, down, up, down! It's not surprising that Marcy reports feeling depressed so often.

Finally we might take a look at whether food sensitivities or allergies may be involved in Marcy's depression. In Marcy's case this is possible, though unlikely. Some research indicates a relationship between depression and lead toxicity, but this is often accompanied by other symptoms which Marcy does not have. Other mental health problems, such as Attention Deficit Disorder and learning disorders, are more likely to be related to food sensitivities and allergies.

Given what we know about Marcy's diet and depression, what can she do?

1. She can reduce her sugar intake including her intake of simple carbohydrates like soft drinks, candy, pastries and even white rice and white bread.

2. She can eliminate caffeine from her diet. This means eliminating caffeinated sodas and coffee.

3. She can modify her diet to include foods that contain some of the B vitamins we mentioned as well as Folic Acid and Vitamin C. In addition to modifying her diet, she might consider taking a vitamin supplement, particularly a B-complex vitamin and Vitamin C. Folic Acid is commonly included in many B-complex supplements.

4. She can begin an exercise program. As discussed earlier, regular exercise can have a dramatic effect on mood and energy levels.

5. Though she is not a heavy drinker, she can eliminate social drinking since alcohol can have the effect of maintaining or exacerbating depression.

6. She may also find it prudent to be screened for lead poisoning and to have a thyroid test. Depression is a common symptom of low thyroid and, according to research published in the Archives of Internal Medicine (February, 2000) there is evidence that up to ten percent of us may suffer from thyroid problems without knowing it.

All of these steps are strategies for Marcy to use her body to influence her mind. She may need some help to implement these strategies successfully. A nutritionist may be able to help her modify her diet and discuss vitamin supplementation with her. She may also find guidance from an orthomolecular physician who is qualified to give her a thyroid test and to screen for lead poisoning. A trainer at the local health club may be able to give her some ideas about starting an exercise program. But to make lifestyle changes like the ones listed above requires effort and self-discipline. If Marcy is willing to work hard and can succeed in making these types of changes, it will not only impact on her feelings of depression, but in all likelihood will make her stronger, healthier and more attractive.

Marcy's experience with traditional therapy has taught her that the solution to her problems is not likely to come from talking with someone in an office or taking medication. Neither of these options has worked for her and both have costs as well as risks. She may find it helpful to reconsider her experience with depression from a completely different viewpoint -- one in which she develops new skills (such as coexisting with depressed feelings), mobilizes her body through diet and exercise, and identifies and clarifies purposes which will give her life meaning. Moving forward on all three fronts, it's likely that Marcy's depression will be addressed as a by-product of a healthier, more skillful, more meaningful and more constructive life. The process of making these types of changes is not easy, but what's at stake is worth the effort.

I've used depression as an example of one mental health problem that may be treatable, in part, by changes in one's diet. But many other psychological disorders may be related to diet and nutrition. While psychiatric medication often produces side effects and can pose long-term risks that are not clear, changes in diet can generally have a positive effect on one's body as well as one's mind -- providing a more natural and holistic approach to one's overall mental health.

<u>Practice</u>

1. Give It Up. Eliminate all refined sugar or caffeine for one month and see if there is a difference in your energy level and sense of well-being.

2. Food Appointments. As a way of cutting back on particular foods, try scheduling appointments for eating those foods, and eat only those foods at the appointed times.

<u>Resources</u>

Werbach, Melvyn, M.D. **Nutritional Influences on Mental Illness**. Tarzana, CA: Third Line Press, Inc. 1999

Challem, Jack. **The Food-Mood Solution: All-Natural Ways to Banish Anxiety, Depression, Anger, Stress, Overeating, and Alcohol and Drug Problems – and Feel Good Again**. Wiley, 2008

Hyman, Mark, M.D. **The Ultra-Mind Solution: The Simple Way to Defeat Depression, Overcome Anxiety and Sharpen your Mind**. Scribner, 2010

NUTRITION AND DEPRESSION

❖ Sugar and Mood Volatility

Sugar is one of the major culprits influencing feelings of depression. Sugar (and simple carbohydrates like refined flour) are absorbed quickly and temporarily raise blood sugar levels. Then insulin is released and lowers blood sugar causing a cycle of repeated cravings for more sugar.

"This constant seesaw from high to low mood can account for many episodes of depression," says William Goldwag, M.D. "Inevitably I find that if someone gets away from an addiction to sugar they function much better. . . particularly for people with chronic depression, chronic fatigue syndrome, and chronic immune system dysfunction. These people find that when they modify their diets and get off sugars, their mental functioning improves considerably."

(For further information see **Thirty Thousand Days**, Vol. 5, No. 1 The Sugar Blues by Elizabeth Somer)

❖ Deficiency - Folic Acid

The Institute of Psychiatry in London found that one third of all patients suffering from depression-related symptoms were borderline to clinically deficient in Folic Acid. Their symptoms improved with Folic-Acid supplements. Another study of healthy individuals showed that those with the highest blood levels of Folic Acid also had the best mood, while those with "low to normal" blood Folic Acid levels were more likely to suffer from depression. Folic Acid deficiency is considered one of the most common vitamin deficiencies in the U.S.

❖ Deficiency - B6

Vitamin B6 deficiency has been reported in up to 79% of depressed patients compared to only 29% of other patients. In a study conducted by the USDA Human Nutrition Research Center at Tufts University, more than one out of four depressed patients were deficient in both vitamins B6 and B12.

❖ Alcohol Can Maintain Depression

Alcohol is a central nervous system sedative and tends to maintain depression rather than elevate mood. It also can increase the level of cortisol, which helps cause low blood sugar reactions. According to Gary Null, Ph.D., alcohol decreases the ability of the body to extract nutrients from the food we eat.

❖ Amino Acids

"Clinically, you can divide depressions into two different categories: the apathetic depression where you just can't get interested in or enjoy anything, and the agitated or

anxious depression, where basically you are depressed and nervous. The latter is responsive to increasing serotonin levels and is best treated with tryptophan. Tryptophan is extremely valuable in cases of agitated depression. Apathetic depression is best treated with tyrosine or what we now call acetyltyrosine, and a product called Noraval."

- Dr. Robert Atkins

❖ Underactive Thyroid

Depression is among the symptoms associated with underactivity of the thyroid gland. Most doctors believe that if the results of a blood thyroid test come back normal, this eliminates thyroid as a possible cause of depression. Nutritionally oriented physicians, however, believe the blood tests often miss a significant number of patients, who have such varied symptoms as depression, fatigue, cold intolerance, dry skin, and brain fog, yet also have normal thyroid tests. If they can determine that your basal metabolism rate is low, they may then prescribe very small amounts of thyroid replacement hormone.

LIVING ON PURPOSE

There was a man who died and found himself in a beautiful place, surrounded by every conceivable comfort. A white-jacketed man came to him and said, "You may have anything you choose: any food, any pleasure, any kind of entertainment."

The man was delighted, and for days he sampled all the delicacies and experiences of which he had dreamed on Earth. But one day he grew bored with all of it, and calling the attendant to him, he said, "I'm tired of all this. I need something to do. What kind of work can you give me?" The attendant sadly shook his head and replied, "I'm sorry, sir. That's the one thing we can't do for you. There is no work here for you."

To which the man answered, "That's a fine thing. I might as well be in hell."

The attendant said softly, "Where do you think you are?"

- Margaret Stevens

At the beginning of some of my workshops I will ask people to reflect on their three most important accomplishments of the past year. I've been asking people this question for the past twenty years and there are two aspects of their answers that strike me as important. First, a significant number of people have trouble identifying three accomplishments. When they reflect on the past year, they can't think of what they did that was important. Second, many people list "having survived" as one of their accomplishments. Under certain circumstances – a war, an intractable illness, being taken hostage – survival is indeed a true accomplishment. But in most cases what people are saying is that their lives are so busy, so chaotic, so overwhelming, that they managed to get through the year without everything falling apart. I have compassion for people in such situations, because it's familiar territory for me. But I also know that survival isn't a purpose that generally offers meaning and fulfillment. Survival usually means that we failed to identify or focus on what truly matters to us. And survival is something that eventually we all fail at – none of us will survive. We need to find a way to go beyond survival and do something that gives our life real meaning.

I've had the privilege of knowing many people who are living purposeful lives. Some are friends, some colleagues -- all are teachers, in their own way. It's no coincidence that they are also some of the most fulfilled people I know. I would characterize their lives as active, focused (often to an extreme), and purposeful. But their lives are more than just purposeful. They are dedicated to purposes which are larger than themselves, which transcend their own self-centered interests. And it is this type of purpose which gives their lives true meaning.

I've also had the opportunity to know people whose lives were relatively purposeless. Of course they have things to do, like laundry, food shopping, and changing the oil in the car. But these activities are devoted primarily to perpetuating their existence. Some are retired, others are mentally ill; some are on welfare while others are quite wealthy. The challenge they face is to find something meaningful to do with their lives. Not coincidentally, I believe, many of these people also struggle with psychological and emotional problems. A lack of purpose means their minds are free to focus on themselves --- their feelings, their thoughts, their body problems, their self-image, and any manner of personal struggle they experience. Their purpose, as it appears to onlookers, is to take care of themselves. They are often preoccupied with the pursuit of their own happiness, which means, more often than not, that they are preoccupied with the lack of happiness in their present circumstances. For such people, purpose and meaning are missing ingredients. They need a good reason to get up in the morning. We all do.

"Many persons have a wrong idea of what constitutes real happiness. It is not obtained through self-gratification but through fidelity to a worthy purpose."

- Helen Keller

OBSTACLES TO LIVING ON PURPOSE

The three most common obstacles to living purposefully are:

1. We have no clear purpose.

Imagine waking up in the morning and having nothing to do. If your life is busy and full of activity, this may seem like a dream come true. But chances are that, after a while, it would probably feel dreadful. Without work to do, friends or family to care for, or a way of being of service in the world, your life might take on an empty quality. Of course you could find things to do. You could take a walk or make a cup of coffee. You could watch TV or surf the Internet. But for most people this would not be a very satisfying life.

Viktor Frankl, the psychiatrist who was imprisoned in a Nazi concentration camp, survived and ultimately developed a method of psychotherapy called Logotherapy. In his book, ***The Doctor and the Soul***, he wrote,

"I remember my dilemma in a concentration camp when faced with a man and a woman who were close to suicide; both had told me that they expected nothing more from life. I asked both my fellow prisoners whether the question was really what we expected from life. Was it not, rather, what life was expecting from us? I suggested that life was awaiting something from them. In fact, the woman was being awaited by her child abroad, and the man had a series of books which he had begun to write and publish but had not yet finished."

Frankl's own survival of the concentration camp was ultimately based on his sense of purpose. His book manuscript was taken from him when he was sent to the camp and he felt it was important to publish that book. His wife was also sent to a different concentration camp and he knew that if she survived he must be there to support her. It was the power of these purposes that helped him bear the torture of life in the camp and survive. In both cases, the question was not what he wanted, but what the world wanted from him. His experience gives us important clues about how to find purpose in our own lives. He later wrote,

"Being human always points, and is directed, to something, or someone, other than oneself -- be it meaning to fulfill or another human being to encounter. The more one forgets himself -- by giving himself to a cause to serve or another person to love -- the more human he is and the more he actualizes himself."

Not everyone will have a grand purpose such as finding a cure for AIDS or eliminating starvation in developing countries. Your purpose may be bringing a child into the world, caring for a pet, or maintaining a section of trail in the national forest. You may have several important purposes that are meaningful to you and those purposes may change as your life evolves.

2. The purposes we have are not meaningful.

Here is a different scenario. Imagine that you work eight hours each day and your job is to dig a deep ditch one day and then fill it in the next day. You are active, you work hard, and you are always busy. Yet it's hard to imagine that such a job would provide any sense of fulfillment. Soon we would begin to question the value of continuing to do this work, even if it paid quite well.

It is not enough just to keep busy. You can be busy and simply do a good job of accomplishing the wrong things. There are a growing number of "downshifters" in our society - people who are trading high-paying jobs for low-paying jobs which they find meaningful. They have discovered that power, fame, or accumulation of wealth, are not purposes which provide fulfillment. As Janet Tallman describes:

"Somewhere in mid-career, as I was developing myself as a professor and anthropologist, I became aware that work without spirit was hollow. Success, money and ambition had carried me to a certain point, but in my early thirties I became overwhelmed with my work's lack of genuine meaning. In retrospect, I have come to understand that what I lacked was devout intention, a commitment to working for purposes which transcend the needs of the day."

In the above quote Tallman uses the phrase "transcends the needs of the day" to describe how easily we can get caught up in the tasks of our daily life without stepping back and questioning our purpose. *Is this really what needs to be done and am I the one who should be doing it?* Often it is not until we are physically removed from our normal environment by taking a vacation or going on retreat that we see our life from a different perspective. Quaker writer Douglas Steere suggests that "work without contemplation is never enough."

Cecil Haynes began working for the Panama Canal when he was 15 years old. He sharpened pencils and refilled inkwells. That was 72 years ago and in all those years he never took a sick day or started a shift late. He became an inventory manager who experienced a change of employers when the U.S. transferred the canal to Panama. Why did he stay at the canal all those years? What made his work meaningful enough to stick with it? Haynes is passionately dedicated to the canal, largely to honor his father, a Barbados-born laborer who helped build the canal beginning in 1904. Almost 22,000 people died building the canal -- from disease, accidents, and landslides. Haynes saw his job as meaningful because it was a way to help insure that the efforts of those men would be remembered.

"My father, and all the others, instilled in me that I should respect their efforts and the labor they put into the canal -- it was part of their lives and we lost a lot of people while building it -- and in memory of those men that I should always try to stay with the canal and do what I could to keep it as one of the wonders of the world."

3. We have purpose, but we fail to act appropriately because of our feelings.

Sometimes we just forget our real purpose. This is often the case with family conflicts. Two people begin arguing and they forget their fundamental purpose (for example, to have a loving marriage) and act in a way that hurts and upsets the other. We become so caught up in the argument that we act as if our purpose was to win the argument at all costs. Rabbi Harold Kushner addresses this situation when he states,

"The purpose of life is not to win. The purpose of life is to grow and share. When you come to look back on all that you have done in life, you will get more satisfaction from the pleasure you have brought into other people's lives than you will from the times that you outdid and defeated them."

Even when our purposes are clear and meaningful, we can fail to move forward because we allow feelings of anxiety, fear, or confusion to derail us. It is often difficult to resist our feelings. But in many cases, making decisions exclusively based on feelings leaves us feeling worse -- at least in the long run.

When it comes to the important purposes of our lives, we can easily be distracted by our feelings. We end up spending more time in front of the TV than we do with our children. We spend more energy shopping for "stuff" than we do meditating or praying. We have short-term passionate affairs, even though they jeopardize our marriage and family. Living on purpose often means co-existing with our feelings while taking action in a constructive direction. This is one of the skills I discussed in the beginning of this book. Our skills are applied in service of a larger purpose.

Even if we have clear and meaningful purposes, we need to make them a reality through realistic effort and action. If we don't, we are unlikely to achieve our purposes. They simply remain ideas in our minds which dissolve each time we succumb to our feelings and abandon the purposes that give life meaning. Finding or discovering life purposes is truly a wonderful gift. But to become reality, big purposes need little actions. And action often involves risk.

Taking Risks

Most of us live life in a way that is designed to maintain the status quo. We live in the same home. Work at the same job. We occupy our leisure time with the same hobbies. Some of us even vacation in the same place each year. We try to fill our lives with the "known" and avoid the unexpected, comforted by the illusion of safety and security that our routine provides. Life ceases to be an adventure where we discover the "new" because we're too busy working through our to-do lists to pause and reconsider how we're using our precious time – our precious life.

We are surrounded by a society that continuously reminds us not to take risks. Risks are bad. Risks are dangerous. Save your money for an emergency. Get an extended warranty on your purchase. Don't drive in bad weather. And make sure you have insurance -- on your car, your home, your flight, your health, and, of course, your life. Our culture encourages us to play it safe. And sometimes that's a good idea. Seat belts, safe sex, backing up your hard drive and bicycle helmets all can provide real benefits. The problem occurs when security dominates our vision of life and leaves no room for taking risks

Richard Leider, author of ***The Power of Purpose***, interviewed more than 1,000 senior citizens, asking them to reflect on their lives. Three themes surfaced in their comments. Leider summarizes them as follows:

"First, they say that if they could live their lives over again, they would be more reflective. They got so caught up in the doing, they say, that they often lost sight of the meaning. Looking back, they wish they had stopped at regular intervals to look at the big picture. Second, if they could live their lives over again, they would take more risks. Almost all of them said they felt most alive when they took risks. And third, if they could live their lives over again, they would understand what really gave them fulfillment. . . . the power of purpose: doing something that contributes to life, adding value to life beyond yourself."

Reflection, risk and contribution – three pillars to a meaningful life. Perhaps we can better express it in an equation:

$$Reflection + Risk = Contribution.$$

Contribution is often the outcome of taking time to reflect and then taking action that usually involves risk. If we study the lives of admirable people we often find that there was a point, or several, where they were willing to forego security and stability to step into the unknown. They traded predictability for risk. .

Albert Schweitzer was one of those people. At the age of 30 he was already a famous theologian and philosopher and was fast becoming an acclaimed musician as well. A logical path lay before him – one of comfort, social status and notoriety. Then, on Friday, October 13, 1906 he mailed a number of letters to family and friends, announcing his decision to study medicine and to leave as soon as possible for Africa. Could he possibly succeed in starting a new career in medicine and moving to the jungle? His friends and family came out, almost universally, against his decision. They argued that he was throwing away all his success and achievements for some preposterous adventure. It was a traumatic time for Schweitzer, but nothing could shake him. He simply said *"J'irai!"* (I'm going).

As Kierkegaard said, "to venture causes anxiety, not to venture is to lose oneself."

I periodically take time to step back and reflect on my life and I've discovered something interesting:

Nearly everything I reflect on that stands out as meaningful involved taking moderate to big risks. Moving to Vermont and starting the ToDo Institute, working with refugee children in Thailand, adopting two children from Asia, starting a new publication (*Thirty Thousand Days*), and homeschooling my children – each of these endeavors required me to step away from the security of the status quo and to jump into the unknown. I had to go outside of my comfort zone. I had to attempt something for which I had little or no experience. I had to have faith.

"Ironically, those who play it safe may be in the greatest danger. When we don't take risks we get stuck in a rut of safety. Over time, we become trapped inside our own life, like a pearl confined to its shell. Life becomes stale and boring. We grow resentful at ourselves for letting our grand passions languish. We tell ourselves, there's got to be something more out there for me. But we know we'll never find it unless we take more risks."

- Bill Treasurer

As I get older, I find my inclination is to take less risk, particularly with the presence of two daughters in my life. It's very tempting to take the safest path. To do the thing that is the least threatening to one's safety, security and comfort. Here's a passage from Gregg Levoy's book, ***Callings: Finding and Following an Authentic Life*** . . .

"Nature places a simple constraint on those who leave the flock to go their own way," says David Bayles and Ted Orland in Art and Fear – 'They get eaten!' "In society, it's a bit more complicated, but the admonition stands: avoiding the unknown has considerable survival value. Society and nature . . . tend to produce guarded creatures. "The upshot is that we often end up trading our authenticity for what we perceive as survival, terrified to swap security for our heart's deep desires, which is the imperative of all callings and one of the dominant fears in responding to them."

So now as callings, dreams, ideas and plans begin to unfold in our minds and hearts we feel the sting of their associated risks. The safe path tempts us with the promise of survival. For animals, survival and procreation are generally the main purposes. But as human beings, most of us want more than survival. We want meaning. We want fulfillment. And that requires risk.

Alex Haley, the highly acclaimed author of Roots, once said about taking risks,

"Nothing is more important. Too often we are taught how not to take risks. When we are children in school, for example, we are told to respect our heroes, our founders, the great people of the past. We are directed to their portraits hanging on walls and in hallways and reproduced in textbooks. What we are not told is that

these leaders, who look so serene and secure in those portraits, were in fact rule-breakers. They were risk-takers in the best sense of the word; they dared to be different."

If you are going to take some risks, then you are likely to be accompanied by an unwelcome partner – fear!

FEAR

When we are seeking to make a significant change in our life we are often faced with the uncertainty of the future. What will happen if I move to North Carolina? Can I get by financially if I go back to school? Can we continue to travel and enjoy the world if we have children? Because the future isn't knowable, we often have thoughts and feelings about what will happen, but those thoughts and feelings don't represent reality, they are simply ideas. Or, as Zen master Ushiyama Roshi, calls them, *secretions in our head*.

Sometimes our fear is providing us with needed wisdom. When I am driving on icy roads during a Vermont snowstorm my attention is riveted to what I'm doing. Fear wakes me up and reminds me to be cautious, attentive and sensitive to the road and the vehicle. If I were too relaxed and unconcerned I might be more likely to get distracted and have an accident. On other occasions my fear is ungrounded and unhelpful. So a good question to ask is "Is there something fear is telling me to do that is a wise response to the situation?"

The Japanese psychiatrist, Shoma Morita, had an unusual view about unpleasant feelings like fear and anxiety. He suggested that fear was simply the "other side of the coin" of our desire to succeed. If we really desire to be safe, then we are likely to be fearful of threats to our safety. If we really want to do well in a job interview, we are likely to be anxious about the interview. Most of us see fear as one thing and the desire to live and be safe as a different thing. But Morita saw them all as the *same* thing – they just manifested themselves differently in different circumstances.

So when we experience fear, we have to recognize it as a healthy expression of our desire to live and be safe. Of course proceeding cautiously may be important and wise to do, depending on the circumstances, but we don't need to give fear the upper hand. We can simply accept it – coexist with it -- and move forward with our purpose, allowing fear to mobilize our attention and energy, just like it does when driving in a snowstorm.

So as you move into the next year of your life, will you be willing to take a risk in order to discover and live out your purpose? There's really not a safe way to do this. If you want to learn to dive, at some point you need to jump into the water. It's a long way down. You won't do it perfectly the first time, or even the second. Make friends with fear and anxiety, for they're likely to join you on your adventure. And nagging self-doubt is normal -- most people have doubts when they venture into something new. Confidence generally develops after we are successful with our efforts, not before. Be wary of plans which involve long waits – retirement or when the kids are all in college. We don't even know what our situation will be tomorrow, let alone five years from now.

The biggest risk you can take is to do nothing at all, when you know you should do something. It may not seem like a big risk right now, but it may result in heartbreaking regret later on when it is too late to move forward with your dreams. When you've reached the end of your life, it's a tragedy if you look back only to regret what you didn't do.

Perhaps this next year of life should come with a warning label:

WARNING: Inaction and security may be hazardous to your purpose!

Let's All Be Composers!

Just follow these simple instructions:

1. *Declare your intention to create a "composition."*

2. *Start a piece at some time.*

3. *Cause something to happen over a period of time (it doesn't matter what happens in your 'time hole' – we have critics to tell us whether it's any good or not, so we won't worry about that part).*

4. *End the piece at some time (or keep it going, telling the audience it is a 'work in progress').*

5. *Get a part time job so you can continue to do stuff like this.*

- Frank Zappa

Practice

1. Naikan Retreat. Naikan self-reflection can help you discover your purpose and also cultivate a profound sense of gratitude for your life. Participants engage in a week of intensive reflection on their lives and relationships with others. This is one of the most potentially transformative experiences available – both psychologically and spiritually.

2. Life and Death Examination

In Playing Ball on Running Water, author David Reynolds suggests writing your epitaph, obituary and eulogy in order to examine long-term purposes and goals. The eulogy will generally be the longest of the three items and will require you to consider the most important elements of your life from the vantage point of the end of your life. What legacy will you leave to the world? What would you have liked to do that you didn't do? What activities were a waste of precious time? Allow at least an hour for this exercise.

3. Assessment of Meaning and Risk.

Reflect on the adult years of your life. First, make a list of what gave your life meaning. It may have been having children, writing a book, or being with your mother when she died. Then make a comparable assessment of the risks you took for each of these meaningful elements of your life. Finally, consider the next phase of your life and think about what might give your life meaning and what you would have to risk.

Resources

Frankl, Viktor. **Man's Search for Meaning**. New York: Simon & Schuster, 1959.

Leider, Richard. **The Power of Purpose**. Berrett-Koehler, 1997, 2010.

Levoy, Gregg. **Callings: Finding and Following an Authentic Life.** Three Rivers Press, 1997.

"We constantly seek a safe little haven in the middle of the hurricane of life. There is no such place. Life is really about simply living and enjoying whatever comes up. Because we have ego-centered minds, however, we think that life is about protecting ourselves. And that keeps us entrapped. An ego-mind is self-centered. It spends its time thinking about how it's going to survive and be safe, comfortable, entertained, pleased, nonthreatened at every juncture. When we live in this way, we've missed the boat."

- Charlotte Joko Beck

Keep Your Feet Moving

There's a story that comes from the Tibetan Buddhist tradition about a young man who has been in spiritual training for several years with his teacher. He is about to embark on one of the most important tests of his training. He must enter a room which is pitch black, make his way through the room and find the exit door. In the room there are demons, and each demon represents one of his greatest fears. As he prepares to enter, his teacher offers him two pieces of advice:

"First, remember that the demons aren't real. But when you encounter them they will seem real. So you must maintain a presence of mind and know, even as you are filled with fear, that the demons are not real."

"And what is the other piece of advice, my teacher?"

"No matter what happens, keep your feet moving. If you keep your feet moving, eventually you will find the way out. But if you stop moving, your attention will be absorbed by fear and it will be hard to get your body moving again."

The student took the teacher's advice and entered the room. Horrifying demons, transforming themselves into his fears, swarmed at him and surrounded him. At times, he forgot his master's first piece of advice and thought they must be real. But he kept his feet moving. And he found the way out.

QUESTIONING ASSUMPTIONS ABOUT MENTAL HEALTH

On the following page I have listed ten questionable assumptions which are commonly made about mental health. Many of these assumptions are accepted as truth in the established mental health system, so they are no longer questioned or investigated. The result is that we pursue strategies and methods which are not always helpful. I have touched on some of these issues in this book. Others require a level of research and inquiry that is outside the scope of this book. I encourage you to approach these assumptions, as well as those you find underlying my own assertions, with an inquiring mind. Test these assumptions with your own direct experience. Create a personal model of mental wellness grounded in your personal experience. Discover, for yourself, a path of knowledge which separates myth from truth.

TEN MYTHS ABOUT MENTAL HEALTH

1. You need to get in touch with feelings you don't know you have.

2. It is important to examine the ways you have been hurt or mistreated in the past.

3. You need to understand why you do what you do in order to change what you do.

4. Expressing your feelings is a way to release or get rid of them.

5. Most mental health problems are biochemical imbalances that need to be treated with medication.

6. It is necessary to acquire self-esteem or confidence before you can take action or change how you are living.

7. You can control your feelings directly by your will.

8. Your diet and exercise choices have no impact on your mental health.

9. All medications approved by the FDA are safe.

10. You have a personality which can be accurately described, diagnosed and labeled.

The ToDo Institute is a non-profit educational organization and retreat center. We offer a variety of publications and programs -- both residential and distance learning – and provide a credit-based program for Certification in Japanese Psychology. For information on training programs, membership, books, or subscriptions to *Thirty Thousand Days - A Journal for Purposeful Living* contact:

ToDo Institute

PO Box 50

Monkton, Vermont 05469

Phone:

800-950-6034

802-453-4440

email: todo@todoinstitute.com

Web site address:

www.todoinstitute.org

ToDo Institute's Distance Learning Courses

Each course lasts thirty days and includes written resources, a central course website with online readings, audio and video, access to a course advisor and a discussion forum for sharing ideas and comments with the learning community.

Living On Purpose
A course to help you find your purpose and then stay on track by helping you clarify priorities and what gives your life meaning.

Renewing Your Relationship
A course to help you redirect energy into your primary relationship -- cultivating a shared vision and a sense of gratitude for your partner.

Working with Your Attention
A course that teaches you how to work more skillfully with your attention and helps you shift away from self-focus, so you can use your attention to be more present in the world.

Taking Action
In this course you select a project that is unfinished or unstarted and use the strategies and support in the course to help you make meaningful progress.

A Month of Self-reflection
A month devoted to self-reflection and cultivating an authentic sense of gratitude for your life. Based on Gregg Krech's book on Naikan and scheduled for the Thanksgiving season.

For information and course schedules contact the ToDo Institute at todo@todoinstitute.com
(802) 453-4440   www.todoinstitute.org

Naikan: Gratitude, Grace and the Japanese Art of Self-Reflection. Berkeley: Stone Bridge Press, 2002.

The Concise, Little Guide to Getting Things Done

(with Linda Anderson Krech)

Middlebury, VT: ToDo Institute, 2001.

A Finger Pointing to the Moon: A workbook for establishing direction and focus in daily life.

(with Linda Anderson Krech)

Middlebury, VT: ToDo Institute, 1996.

Life is a Matter of Attention

Audio CD program -- 90 minutes

ToDo Institute

To purchase call

(800) 950-6034 or (802) 453-4440

todo@todoinstitute.com

www.todoinstitute.org